SMALL-GROUP WRITING CONFERENCES, K–5

SMALL-GROUP WRITING CONFERENCES, K–5

How to Use Your Instructional Time More Efficiently

Holly Slaughter

HEINEMANN
PORTSMOUTH, NH

Heinemann
361 Hanover Street
Portsmouth, NH 03801–3912
www.heinemann.com

Offices and agents throughout the world

Library of Congress Cataloging-in-Publication Data

Slaughter, Holly.
    Small-group writing conferences, K–5 : how to use your instructional time more efficiently / Holly Slaughter.
        p.   cm.
    Includes bibliographical references.
    ISBN-13: 978-0-325-01736-5
    ISBN-10: 0-325-01736-0
    1. English language—Composition and exercises—Study and teaching (Elementary). 2. Group work in education. 3. Elementary school teaching. I. Title.
    LB1576.S578   2009
    372.62'3044—dc22
                                             2008048279

Editor: Kate Montgomery
Production editor: Sonja S. Chapman
Cover design: Jenny Jensen Greenleaf
Cover photograph: Nick Doll Photography
Compositor: Newgen North America
Manufacturing: Steve Bernier

Printed in the United States of America on acid-free paper
13 12 11 10 09   PAH   1 2 3 4 5

To Tim, Ella, and Emersyn:
my most intense and gratifying small group

Contents

SECTION FOUR   VALUABLE RESOURCES

Acknowledgments

"Everything you do begins and ends with relationships." A good friend taught me that. I am especially thankful for the relationships I have with my family, friends, and colleagues.

Thank you first to my favorite small group. To Ella, my sweet, sweet Ella. For sitting next to me late one night as I pecked away at my laptop proclaiming, "If your book is published, Mom, I'll buy one!" And for Emme, pumpkin-pie Emme. For reminding me not to infringe too much on family time by plunking your head down in my lap begging, "Let's play the tickle-the-pits game!" How can anyone refuse the tickle-the-pits game? To Tim, my husband, friend, and colleague, thank you for knowing the little things that matter most to me. I'm especially thankful for the weekend mornings when you allow me to lie in bed and pretend that I don't hear the girls stirring as you get up and close the bedroom door behind you.

Thanks to my parents, Joseph and Margo, and Penelope Tobias for raising me to believe in endless possibilities. Along with my grandmother, Barbara Wallis, you instilled in me a love for reading and for language, a passion for thinking, and a desire for laying out ideas for conversation and debate. And does our family love to debate! Thank you for supporting, and especially for believing, that teaching children is the noblest profession there is. Thank you also to my brother, Noel (and Tina too!), and for my family, Frank and Karen Slaughter, for your excitement and support surrounding this project.

For my bestest friends in the whole wide world: Gina, Colleen, Lisa, Robin, Dea, Christy, Larissa, and Becky. Thanks for understanding when I couldn't be there. And thanks for being there when I could.

Thank you to Nick Doll of Nick Doll Photography for helping me "tell my story" with pictures. Thanks mostly for your professionalism and ease in working with students.

Thank you to my developmental editor, Kerry Herlihy. Your close reading of my early drafts helped me rethink the structure and shape of my book. In a *very* short time I learned to trust you, respect your ideas, and know you as a friend.

Thank you to Sonja Chapman, Production Editor, for orchestrating all things necessary in the production process. Your deadlines and efficiency were a blessing during the last leg of this process.

And a special thank-you to my editor Kate Montgomery, *the* Kate Montgomery . . . let me just begin by saying that well over a year ago, I checked my phone messages to find a message from you on my phone. Well, I did what any respectable Heinemann groupie would do: I screamed bloody murder and dropped the phone on the floor! Having read so many books with your name imprinted on them, I couldn't believe I was so fortunate to have you as my editor. Besides the fact that you are brilliant, your openhearted responses, insights, and energy for this project inspired some of my most thoughtful revisions. I am a better writer and my book is enormously better because of your close attention to detail and unique vision for honing in on exactly what readers will want. And for the record, over a year later I *still* have that first message saved on my voice mail!

I owe a thousand thanks to the teachers at Rawlings Elementary School in Pinellas Park, Florida. As early pioneers in this work, you trudged through repeated practices—"Try this!" and "Now, try this!" The revolutionary work we began during seminar and in your classrooms is the framework on which this book is built.

I have been blessed to work alongside many teachers in Pinellas County Schools. I especially want to thank the teachers and students at Shore Acres Elementary, Orange Grove, Bear Creek, and Rawlings who welcomed me in their classrooms. The contributions of these teachers spurred further thinking and revised practice. Although many teachers have helped shape my thinking, I must individually thank the teachers whose ideas, and oftentimes names, appear in the pages of this book. A *huge* thanks to: Rachel Tracy, Tracy Smith, Laura Roe, Kathy Casey, Jennifer Pellerin, Courtney Claud, Telsha Marmash,

Courtney Rasmussen, Heather Dragon, Barrie Evans, Debbie Chin, Annette Robinson, Connie Lance, Jan Pittenger, Lynn Stevens, Annette Pagliaro, Lisa Cotilla, Vanessa Bowen, Jennifer McCafferty, Tonja Wilson, Michelle Betz, Whisper Wiseman, Janice Schomburg, Danielle Cicalese, Kim Stang, Cecilia Summerall, Kim Stauffer, and Allison Lucente.

I am grateful also for my fellow staff developers, past and present, who have offered specific ideas, encouragement, and advice: Gail Ramsdell, Nancy Weiffenbach, Doug Henson, Paige Michael, Kathy Beauregard, Connie Dierking, and Michelle Gallagher. Thank you also to Leesa Pearson and Cathy Torres for coleading the research project that brought me to my first visit to Teachers College years ago.

To Roy Peter Clark for inventing writers camp, where small-group work has been a mainstay for the last twenty-five years, and for allowing me to be a part of it. Thank you also for meeting with me during this process and answering my questions—"Can you talk to me about the arc of a book?"

I must acknowledge a group of people, some of whom I've never met, but by either reading their words or hearing them speak, they have shaped my beliefs and attitudes about the teaching of writing: Donald Murray, Don Graves, Lucy Calkins, Katie Wood Ray, Ralph Fletcher, Georgia Heard, and *especially* Amanda Hartman and Maggie Moon.

I am so grateful for my colleagues, Mary Hosford and Carolyn Glass, for ongoing support and friendship. You have been wonderful writing partners. Carolyn, you've read drafts, given feedback, offered advice. Mary, you've done all of those things *and* taken my calls late at night, letting me know, "I'll be up till eleven or so if you need to call me back."

To Christy Curran, my former colleague, and dear friend, I am so grateful for you. Even though you moved to New York City (I'm still not over it, you know), thank you for being just a phone call away. Your time, feedback, ideas, and excitement have been invigorating and invaluable.

Each December, before we break for two weeks, I sit down at my dining room table to write holiday cards to my colleagues. Every December, it seems, I save the same card for last. It's not because I have *nothing* to say. It's because I have *everything* to say, and I just don't know where to begin. I sit and stare at the blank card hoping something clever will come to me. Nothing does. I finally tell myself, "Get on with it!" and year after year I find myself beginning with those same first two words: *Dear Mary.* And so my final thanks, and most difficult, is for my mentor, my friend, Mary Osborne. When I was a young teacher, you came in to my classroom and I watched you teach my fourth graders writing. I marveled and said to myself, "I want to be her. I want to have *that* effect on my kids." You became my benchmark for teaching and still are to this day. Later, I left the classroom to work alongside you—well, sort of. You were my S.O.B. (sort of boss) and fellow writing staff developer, and I have tried to follow in your footsteps. Because you have mentored me, nurtured me, and brought out things in me I never even dreamed possible, more than anyone else, I hope that *you* read this book and it makes you proud. Without you, none of this would be possible. Professional relationship aside, I am blessed to call you my friend. How many times you have demonstrated through your actions that at the heart of everything you do and say are the relationships you keep. Thank you for teaching me the most important life lesson, my dear friend Mary Osborne, "Everything you do begins and ends with relationships."

Introduction

In Florida, we return to school during the last week of July, still beating the summer sand out of our flip-flops on the way into the building. Four summers ago, I returned to my profession as refreshed, relaxed, and renewed as I had the previous ten.

But that year was different, because it was my first year in unfamiliar territory. I had left the classroom and become a writing staff developer. It was my job to work side by side with kindergarten through fifth-grade teachers, coaching them during writing workshop. That same year our district implemented new "units of study" as our writing curriculum, and I was the "expert." I certainly didn't feel like an expert. In my ten years as a classroom teacher, I had taught third, fourth, and fifth graders. In this new position, I provided staff development to kindergarten and first- and second-grade teachers, as well. Thankfully, I was able to spend many of my professional development days in primary classrooms watching and practicing alongside teachers I admired and trusted.

One of those teachers was Jan Pittenger. My first morning in Jan's room, I watched in awe as she taught her kindergarten students a writing minilesson. I watched her confer. Then I went off to confer with Sam while Jan conferred with Nazir. Close enough to overhear each other, we soon realized we were having the same conference! At first, I was just thrilled to be thinking along the same lines as Jan, who had been teaching kindergarten for twenty years. Jan, the master kindergarten teacher—the master writing teacher.

Later Jan and I talked about the similarities of our conferences and the similarities of the students' needs. Wouldn't it have been just as effective to confer with Nazir and Sam at the same time? Could any other students in the room that day have benefited from that same conference?

I became fascinated by the predictable patterns I saw emerging in the classrooms in which I worked. Students struggled with the same strategies and experienced the same successes. Teachers often repeated the same conference over and over.

In talking with me about their work, teachers asked the same questions: "How do I manage conferring with twenty-five or thirty students? How many students should I meet with every day? Each week? How often should I meet with my struggling students? I'm only able to meet with a handful of students each week—is this enough?"

I began to wrap my brain around the idea of small-group work inside the writing workshop. At a summer writers camp I co-coordinate at the Poynter Institute for Media Studies, in St. Petersburg, Florida, teachers and children have been working together in small groups for twenty-five years. But that's *camp.* Could this approach transfer to the classroom?

The previous summer, I had sat in the chapel of Columbia University's Grace Dodge Hall, a third-grade teacher listening intently to every word Lucy Calkins said, scribbling notes across the pages of my blue hardcover "summer institute" writing notebook. Sharing the latest thinking of the Teachers College Reading and Writing Project about writing workshop, Lucy said, "More and more I'm apt to read over shoulders, tapping a child and then another and another. 'Come with me,' I say. And then I pull together a small group."

I thought. And thought some more. The idea of small-group work in a writing workshop conflicted with what I knew about teaching writing in the classroom and the individualized nature of the writing conference. Doubts quickly made themselves heard: Can this *really* work? How would it go *exactly?* Then a quieter voice whispered, "But we're teaching the writer and not the writing. Couldn't a few children in the class benefit from my instruction on this topic? We recognize the value of teaching small groups in reading and math, so why not writing?" In *The Writing Workshop: Working Through the Hard Parts (And They're All Hard Parts)* (Ray with Laminack 2001), Katie Wood Ray says, "When we sit down next to a student, we bring with us what I call a 'fistful' of knowledge about writing that we draw from to teach this writer." What about the other fist. . . .

And so, the teachers I worked with and I began studying and rethinking instructional approaches during the write-and-confer portion of the writing workshop. We didn't find many resources. There is plenty of research supporting small-group instruction in reading and math, but information specific to small-group instruction in writing is slim. So we set out to answer some questions ourselves.

- When should we form small groups?
- Why should we form small groups?
- How are our small groups like and unlike individual conferences?
- Could small-group instruction replace individual conferences? (The answer is no, by the way.)
- Are there helpful tips for managing small groups? (Absolutely.)
- What can go wrong?
- Will implementing small-group instruction in writing workshop put a heavier burden on already swamped teachers? (No! It's a better way to use the time we already have.)

Small-group instruction is certainly not new. Teachers are very familiar with teaching small groups while other children in the room work independently. However, the ideas in this book are specific to writing and based on a commonsense approach to conferring and meeting with students more efficiently and effectively. The suggestions will help teachers think about the students in their classrooms in terms of similar strengths and needs—to work smarter, not harder. And be assured that conferring with individual students remains an integral part of the writing workshop.

Most assuredly, this isn't a step-by-step program in a box. It doesn't come with daily lesson plans. Teachers who are looking for a highly effective quick-fix approach to the teaching of writing—a day-by-day how-to—will not find it here (or anywhere that I know).

The ideas in this book have been shaped by information gained from the great books on teaching writing: *Writing: Teachers and Children at Work* (Graves 1983, 2003), *What a Writer Needs* (Fletcher 1993), *The Art of Teaching Writing* (Calkins 1994), *How's It Going? A Practical Guide to Conferring with Student Writers* (Anderson 2000), *The Writing Workshop: Working Through the Hard Parts (And They're All Hard Parts)* (Ray with Laminack 2001), *One to*

One: The Art of Conferring with Young Writers (Calkins et al. 2005), to name just a few. They have been developed during productive conversations with teachers, fellow staff developers, and professional writers. They have been enriched by summer institutes at Teachers College. And so many of them first dawned during summer writers camps at the Poynter Institute for Media Studies.

About This Book

The first section provides convincing reasons to meet with small groups of students during the writing workshop. Section 2 offers specific ideas for forming groups in order to meet the diverse needs of your students. Section 3— Chapters 6 through 9, the heart of the book—describes the different kinds of small-group conferences. Each of these chapters contains a classroom snapshot, a discussion of when to conduct this kind of conference, and teaching tips. The final section suggests several ways to record conferences quickly, as well as how to manage issues that will arise in any writing workshop.

The subtitle of Leah Mermelstein's book *Reading/Writing Connections in the K–2 Classroom* (2005) is *Find the Clarity and Then Blur the Lines.* I love that. It makes sense in teaching writing, and in life. I suggest you read about and try in your classroom one group-work structure at a time. Once you understand them and are comfortable implementing them, blur the lines!

Why Is Small-Group Work Necessary?

In my third-grade classroom, I felt a sense of satisfaction when I was able to hold four or five individual conferences a day. That was a lot. But it still wasn't enough. I wanted to meet with all my students at least once a week. And I wanted to meet with my students who struggled more often than that. With no more time to give, I fell short of that goal every day, every week, every month.

After studying conferring in small groups and rethinking instructional approaches during the write-and-confer portion of the writing workshop, I now think we can plan the time we spend conferring in much more ambitious ways. Instead of meeting with four or five students a day, why not with ten or fifteen? I know what you're thinking: *I'm going to need more time*. But the number of conferences can remain the same. We'll just expand our *definition* of conferring to include partnerships and small groups of three or four children.

A Classroom Snapshot

Laura Roe, a second-grade teacher, has just wrapped up her minilesson. Today she launched a brand new unit of study, poetry. She taught her delighted poets how to see the world through the poet's eye: how to take ordinary objects and look at those objects as a poet would, finding beauty and unexpected qualities. Children tiptoe to their table groups. Their poetry folders, writing paper, and freshly sharpened pencils rest momentarily on desks, at the ready. The students begin to write.

Laura pushes a button on the CD player. Soft music fills the room. Then she pulls a chair up to a table group. She has her own poetry folder (just like the ones her students are using), her own poetry paper (just like the paper her students are using), and her own freshly sharpened pencil. She, too, begins to write a poem. After a minute or two, Laura stands up and begins circulating among the students, reading over their shoulders, jotting quick notes on her clipboard.

She pauses next to Raul, who is sitting quietly, a puzzled look on his face, his paper blank. She bends down so that she is on Raul's level. "Raul, how's it going?" Raul says he doesn't know what to write about. Laura smiles and pats him on the shoulder. She reminds him that writers have strategies they use when they face the blank page and that poetry is no different. She has a *one-to-one conference*, reminding Raul of strategies he already knows as a writer. Raul begins to write the first line of his poem. . . .

Laura continues her "research." She reads over shoulders. She smiles warmly. She nods when she passes children who excitedly hold up their poems for her admiration. She gives a thumbs-up to several students and jots a few names on her clipboard.

Quietly, she taps Giovany. "Grab your poem and meet me on the rug," she whispers. She asks Britany to do the same. Jermaine, too. The three children and Laura sit together in a small circle. Laura begins, "I called you all over to the rug because as I was reading over your shoulders, I noticed all of you were working really hard writing poems. I was amazed how much you all have written already. Will each of you hold up your poems so we can admire your work?" Giovany, Britany, and Jermaine proudly do so. "Britany, you've worked really hard on your beach poem. Jermaine, you must be so proud of your back-yard poem. Giovany, I see you are writing a poem about your brother. He's the topic of so much of your writing, isn't he?"

Next, Laura asks the students to place their poems and pencils behind them for a moment and takes her own poem out of her folder. "I wrote this poem today. Then I reread it, and I noticed it doesn't look like a poem or sound like a poem. It looks and sounds just like the stories we were writing last week in our narrative unit. Whenever I write a poem that looks and sounds like a story, I reread it and try to cross out any words that sound like story words—

one time, then, after that—and dull words like *the, and,* or *are.* I try to leave in words that show action, describe feeling, and evoke image. And because I know that poets often work hard to make meaning with fewer words, I try to rewrite my poem in less space, like this." Laura takes a fresh piece of paper out of her folder, folds it in half lengthwise, and demonstrates the work she's described. Then she sums up her teaching point: "You can try this strategy whenever you write poetry. If your poem is starting to look or sound more like a story, you could try eliminating words you don't need and rewriting your poem in shorter lines so that it looks and sounds more like a poem. Let's try this work right here on the rug, shall we?"

As the students in this *skill group conference* try out the strategy on their poems, Laura offers specific suggestions and praise, pointing to places in their writing. Britany uses the strategy independently, while Giovany needs some additional coaching. Once each child is applying the strategy on his or her own, Laura encourages the children to continue working on the rug and tells them she'll be back in a few moments to admire their progress. As she walks away, Giovany, Britany, and Jermaine continue to reread their poems and cross out words.

Laura then approaches the table where Mackenzie is sitting. All five children there are writing poems. Mackenzie is drawing a picture in the box at the top of the paper Laura provided. Once again Laura bends down to eye level. "How's it going, Mackenzie?" Mackenzie looks up at her teacher wide-eyed and explains that she is drawing a part of her poem in the box. Laura replies, "That's really smart work, Mackenzie. You are using a strategy we learned as writers earlier in the year, that if you want to add detail to your writing, something you can do is to sketch."

Laura then begins a *table conference* with all the students sitting at this table. "Poets. May I have your attention? I can see you know what to do when a teacher says, 'May I have your attention?' because your pencils are down and all of your eyes are on me. I want to show you Mackenzie's poem. Do you notice how Mackenzie is using her sketch box? She remembered we learned how writers often make a drawing when they want to add details to their piece. She knows that these strategies we're learning as writers are for anytime we write. We could all try Mackenzie's strategy right now. If you want to add details to your poem, the way Mackenzie did, draw a sketch in your box or add to the one you've already drawn. Then try adding those details to your poem."

The students pick up their pencils and begin sketching. Laura moves around the table, coaching and scaffolding. "I noticed you added polka dots to your beach umbrella in your sketch, Anna. Are you planning on adding that detail to your beach poem? Where do you think it might fit best?"

Leaving the table, Laura decides to check the progress of the skill group on the carpet. As she approaches, Giovany is reading his poem to Britany and Jermaine, who are nodding and smiling. Laura joins them. "I see all of you have rewritten your poem so that it looks and sounds more like a poem. Continue what you were doing, I just want to listen in." Britany reads her poem out loud to the group. Jermaine responds, "I like your poem because it sounds poetic." Britany turns to Laura and smiles.

It's time to wrap up. Laura asks her poets to put their pencils down. Sighs, whines, and clicks of the tongue are heard from every corner of the classroom. As Laura asks everyone to meet on the rug for a share session, she assures them that tomorrow they will write again.

Behind the Snapshot

While the children were writing, Laura met with one student in a one-to-one conference, three students in a skill conference, and five children in a table conference—a total of nine students—without increasing the time she spent on conferences. She was able to meet the needs of more students by changing the *way* she conferred with them. When a change in approach means teachers can have effective and meaningful conferences with ten or fifteen children instead of four or five, that change becomes *necessary*. Small-group instruction:

- contributes to "two-fisted teaching"
- allows us to widen our approach to assessment
- helps us focus on strategy-based instruction
- enriches cooperative learning and provides social benefits

Two-Fisted Teaching

We can think about Katie Wood Ray's apt "fistful" of knowledge not just in terms of one fist but two. In one fist, we hold what we know about writing *content:* genre, topics, structure, focus, elaboration, voice, syntax, conventions, and the like. In the other fist, we hold what we know about our *teaching practices:* ways to engage children, types of instruction, methods of teaching, teaching tools, management techniques, organization and planning, and so forth.

What energized me most about studying and conferring with small groups of children was the growth I experienced as a writing teacher. Exponential growth. When we confer with one child, we usually have their eyes and their attention because of the one-to-one nature. When working with three or four children, we learn to be a little more savvy, engaging all the children in the group at once and holding their attention for a short stretch of time.

With children in a small group, you also receive immediate feedback about the effectiveness of your teaching: *Yippee! They got it. It worked!* Or, *Uh-oh. They're staring at me with blank faces. They are* not *getting it.* Yes, we receive immediate feedback in a one-to-one conference. But let's face it, the feedback can be a little difficult to parse. Was my teaching strategy brilliant and explicit or was the child simply having a moment of brilliance? It's hard to tell. If I teach Manuel that writers use punctuation to bring voice to their writing and Manuel is successful, I'll probably walk away from that conference feeling pretty good about my teaching. If Manuel is not successful, I might think, *That Manuel! If only he would pay careful attention to my teaching!* However, if I teach a small group of students that writers use punctuation to bring voice to their writing and the majority of the students try doing that work and do it successfully—or not—the odds are that the result can be attributed to my explicit teaching method.

Conferring with small groups of children helps us deepen our content knowledge as well. When we teach writing to small groups of children, we tend to think through possibilities as we plan our unit and minilessons: If I teach a minilesson to the whole class (that writers use punctuation to bring voice to their writing, for example), what are the possible responses in this class? And how will I respond to those possibilities? (This is described more fully in Chapter 3.)

I didn't do very much of that kind of thoughtful planning when I only conferred with individuals. I expected to sit down next to a child and teach the child based on our conversation. We would talk a bit, and based on that talk a teaching point would emerge. Although I believe this kind of conferring is valid and important, I am now convinced that the very expectation of teaching small groups of children helps me deepen my thinking and understanding of content knowledge. Let me illustrate.

I meet with Sammy in a writing conference. Sammy reads a part of her story she is particularly proud of because she has added dialogue. As I listen to Sammy tell me about her dialogue, I'm trying to decide what to teach Sammy next. I could teach her that writers don't just add dialogue, they add internal thinking. Or I could teach her that writers insert a comma before the quotation marks. Or that writers add details about the setting. I have tons of choices. And in one-to-one conferences, our choices too often lead us to *something else* rather than help the child *build or deepen the work she or he is already doing.*

Now let's say I've noticed that Sammy, Julian, Sophia, and Manuel have all added dialogue to their pieces. I pull them together as a small group because I noticed they are all doing smart work and I want to help them do even better work. More than likely, I'll teach the group that writers don't add dialogue for the sake of having dialogue but to reveal big, strong feelings of the character. When I expect to teach small groups of children, I think of the content on a continuum. If my students do X, how will I help them do it better?

Studying about and introducing small-group work in writing workshop will expand our practice in ways that support and empower our students and help us become two-fisted teachers. It is *necessary* for our professional growth.

Wider Assessment

As skilled teachers, we informally assess each of our student writers *every day.* We observe him as he writes, we read her pieces, we have conversations with him, we listen to what she tells us. We ask ourselves, What do I know about this child as a writer? What are his strengths? What are her needs? These assessments inform and guide our teaching: we know exactly what a student needs in order to become a better writer. Then, usually at the end of a unit of study, we assess the work of the entire class, collecting all the pieces and using a rubric to score and categorize each one.

Although this is worthwhile, we need to widen our assessment stance, add up what we know about this child *and* this child *and* this child, and ask, "What do I know about this class as writers? What are some patterns of strengths? What are some patterns of needs?" By doing this, we learn valuable information about our class in the *process* of writing. We notice that our students have similar strengths and similar needs. We pull students with similar strengths and needs together as a small group and address those strengths and needs.

In *A Guide to the Writing Workshop,* Units of Study for Teaching Writing, Grades 3–5 (2006), Lucy Calkins writes:

> It is sometimes worthwhile to look over the entire class, thinking, "How are all my children doing in any one area?" For example, we could ask, "How are all my children doing at writing stories in which a character moves sequentially through time?" This will probably result in our gathering clusters of children together and providing each cluster with some small-group strategy lessons. (104)

Planning for and teaching small-group strategy lessons requires teachers to study both individuals and the class as a whole. Teachers become more and more and more skilled by assessing writers every day. By regularly widening our approach to assessment, we deepen our understanding of our children as writers: challenging and *necessary* work.

Strategy-Based Teaching

Each type of small-group conference described in this book builds on an ever growing knowledge of one-to-one conferring. Teachers who have read books by Lucy Calkins and Carl Anderson understand the purpose for a writing conference: to help students become better writers. We want to teach our students strategies they will employ any and every time they write, not just to the piece of writing in front of them. In *How's It Going?* (2000), Carl Anderson writes:

> One way we help students become better writers is by teaching them strategies and techniques more experienced writers use to write well. When we finish a conference, we hope we can say to ourselves, "I taught Erika a

Example 1

Teacher: How's it going?

Student: Good.

Teacher: So it's going good. . . . Stephanie, I see you are working on a story about the bathtub.

Student: Yep.

Teacher: Can you show me what you are working on right now?

Student: Well, I decided to slow down the part where the bubble came out of my mouth. That's the good part of my story. But I'm a little bit . . . stuck.

Teacher: Stuck how?

Student: I don't really know what to write. I'm stuck.

Teacher: Hmmm.

Student: Like how to make that longer.

Teacher: Well, where did the bubble come from?

Student: Shampoo got in my mouth.

Teacher: What happened when the bubble came out of your mouth?

Student: It popped.

Teacher: Yuck.

Student: I washed my mouth out in the faucet sprayer.

Teacher: You could add that the shampoo got in your mouth and that the bubble popped and that you washed your mouth out in the faucet to your story. Try adding those details to your story. . . .

Example 2

Teacher: How's it going?

Student: Good.

Teacher: So it's going good. . . . Stephanie, I see you are working on a story about the bathtub.

Student: Yep.

Teacher: Can you show me what you are working on right now?

Student: Well, I decided to slow down the part where the bubble came out of my mouth. That's the good part of my story. But I'm a little bit . . . stuck.

Teacher: Stuck how?

Student: I don't really know what to write. I'm stuck.

Teacher: Hmmm.

Student: Like how to make that longer.

Teacher: You know something important about writing stories—that we don't give equal weight to all the parts of the story. Some parts we tell quickly. And some parts, especially the parts that hold the big meaning, we slow down and stretch out. There are lots of strategies we can use when stretching out a part of our stories. One that's especially helpful to me when I write is that writers slow down moments by making a movie in their mind. Let me show you what I mean. I try to remember that part of the story like a movie. I close my eyes and I picture it . . . I'll think, "How did it go exactly?"

Figure 1.1   Strategy-Based Example

strategy for spelling an unfamiliar word," or "I taught Jemel how he could use short sentences to create emphasis." By having students try what we teach them in the piece of writing they are currently working on, we give them an opportunity to learn what we've taught so they can use the strategy or technique *for the rest of their writing lives.* (9)

See figure 1.1 for a couple examples. In example 1, the teacher has clearly helped Stephanie with her *writing*. However, has she helped Stephanie become a better *writer*? No. The conversation and teaching never go beyond the particular piece of writing. The teacher does not name a strategy. She asks a series of questions. The student answers her questions. Then the teacher makes an assignment: "Add those details to your story."

The focus, or teaching point, of the conference in example 2 is strategy based. Will the strategy help this particular piece of *writing*? Sure. But more than that, this strategy will help the *writer become a better writer*. Reread the last statement by the teacher. She never mentions the piece of writing. She uses specific language—"writers slow down moments by making a movie in their mind"—to let the child know this is a strategy for anytime you write, not just for today, not just for this piece.

One benefit of conducting small-group conferences in the writing workshop is that the nature of a small group forces teachers to teach the *writer*, not the *writing*. Imagine pulling four students together and carrying on the line of questioning in example 1 with each student in the group. It would be a disaster—not to mention a waste of time. Most of us who have stumbled through the early stages of group work don't have to imagine. We've lived it—been there, done that, don't want to do it again. Conferring with small groups of students helps us get beyond the piece of writing and teach the *writer*.

If we believe our job as writing teachers is to help students become better writers by teaching writing strategies they can use, not just today, but forever and ever, then it is *necessary* to pull small groups together in writing workshop.

Social Impact

In *How's It Going?* Carl Anderson also writes, "A few words, a smile, a nod of understanding. That's all it takes to show students we care about them. That's all it takes to inspire some students to stretch themselves as writers. That's all it takes to change some students' writing lives" (2000, 23). When we talk with children about their writing, we are sending an important message: *I care*. How often do we want to send "I care" messages to our students? As often as possible. Every small-group conference is another opportunity to send another "I care" message—another opportunity for our young writers to stretch themselves and change their lives.

When we meet with small groups of children to talk with them about their writing, we knowingly model the art of conversation:

- listening to one another
- responding to one another
- questioning one another
- coaching one another
- supporting one another
- learning from one another
- celebrating and admiring one another

And the model takes. We know, because we've observed it happen in hundreds of classrooms. When we walk away from a group of students, they'll write for a bit, but inevitably they start talking. They show off their work. They question one another. They ask one another for help. We love it when this happens. We secretly expect it. And sometimes, it's the very reason we're convening the group. We explicitly teach our students how to talk and respond to another writer.

If we believe our job as teachers goes beyond curriculum, if we believe we are much more effective in our work when we nurture relationships with and among the children in our classroom community, if we believe conferences are really conversations in which we have golden opportunities to model ways we can talk to one another, it becomes *necessary* to convene small-group conferences in writing workshop.

Identifying the Essentials

The other day I was talking to my friend Mary Anne. She described her recent success with keeping off the weight she had lost. "I lost twenty-two pounds by eating a low-carb diet. And I've kept it off for over a year."

She had my full attention. "Really? What's your secret?"

"I gave up white foods," she explained, "white rice, potatoes, pasta, white bread."

"What about pizza?" I asked.

"I don't eat it. What good is pizza if you can't eat the crust?"

"Exactly."

And although I cannot imagine my life without pizza, I thought about the truth behind what my friend had said. There are things in life that can't be separated. Like a pizza's sauce and toppings need the crust, the ideas and suggestions presented in this book need the writing workshop, the classroom environment, and units of study.

Writing Workshop

I know no way to teach writing other than in a writing workshop. For me, the workshop is the most essential facet of teaching writing. Every day for between forty-five and sixty minutes, teachers teach writing during a block of time structured in what my colleague Mary Osborne calls the three-circle format: *participating in direct or explicit instruction, writing and conferring,* and *sharing.* This daily structure and rhythm provide both time and space in which to meet with individuals and small groups. We don't have to create centers or activities to keep the students busy while we are occupied with a small group. Rather, students learn strategies that enable them to keep their writing going independently, to do the work of writers.

During explicit instruction, we present a directed minilesson to all the members of the class, who are usually gathered in a central meeting area. The *teaching point* is specific and connected to a *unit of study.*

When it is time to write and confer, students go to their tables or other assigned spots and do the work of writers. We often write alongside a group of students for a minute or two, setting the tone of the workshop and model- ing that we, like them, are writers. We confer with individuals as well as small groups. (Most of the ideas, structures, and methods presented in this book are specific to the write-and-confer portion of the writing workshop.)

During the sharing session, we call the students back to the meeting area and lead a discussion of their work. We might highlight a student or a group of students who tried out the day's teaching point, extended a strat- egy, or exhibited productive independence, using this example as another teaching opportunity. Or partners of small groups might share and discuss their work.

Classroom Environment

A major purpose of the writing workshop is to foster independence. We workshop teachers organize our classrooms carefully. We know we'll need a *meeting area* where students can gather for explicit instruction. Usually, there is a flip chart, markers, mentor texts, and whatever else we need to teach writing.

If we can, we set up the classroom so that children work at tables; this makes it easier to present small-group skill instruction and conduct table conferences. An alternative is to push individual desks together into a table formation. Often we have designated a specific area writing for materials: sharpened pencils in various colors, different types of paper, dictionaries, thesauruses, and anything else students may need.

The classroom walls display relevant writing terms, as well as strategy and process charts created during minilessons, so we and our students can refer to them at will. There may also be a special wall section on which to display student work.

Units of Study

A unit of study is a whole-class study focused on a particular topic or genre. Generally, a unit of study lasts four weeks, although some may be longer, some shorter. The explicit instruction in the minilesson and the one-to-one and small-group conferences support the bigger unit of study. Usually, teachers at a grade level determine the specific units that will make up their yearlong curriculum. Many teachers begin the year by studying personal narrative, then balance out the remainder of the year with fictional narrative, poetry, and informational writing.

I strongly recommend Lucy Calkins' two book series, *Units of Study for Primary Writing* (2007) and *Units of Study for Teaching Writing, Grades 3–5* (2006) for a deeper read on units of study teaching.

I taught writing for many years without being aware of the term *units of study* as it relates to writing workshop. But when I think of conferring in small groups and how it relates to writing units of study, I am reminded of those little wooden Russian nesting dolls that my girls play with every time they go to Grandma and Grandpa's house. One little doll stacks into the next doll and the next and the next. A conference is the doll that stacks inside the next biggest doll, the minilesson. And the minilesson stacks inside the unit of study.

The unit of study stacks inside the yearly curricular calendar, which stacks inside the grade-level meetings. The smaller parts stack up to the whole. Our daily teaching, whether delivered in whole-class minilessons or small-group conferences, needs to stack up within something bigger—a unit of study—that helps us design and focus our teaching.

To obtain the full benefits of this book, you will want to work toward having all these essentials in place. But even without the essentials in place, the book will still help you become better at conferring with small groups of children, as well as conferring in general, and will help you see why these essentials are important.

Predictable Planning

Last year, my oldest daughter entered kindergarten. If you have ever been in a kindergarten classroom on the first day of school, you know it is something to behold. An experienced kindergarten teacher knows how to welcome children and their parents. She knows how to make them feel comfortable. She knows exactly what to do when the children cry. She knows how to respond when the parents cry. She has tissue boxes. She has everything labeled, color-coded, and illustrated. She's a master at maneuvering twenty children (many of whom have never been in a school before) to their spots and at the same time ever so gently easing the parents out of the room so she can begin the year. And through it all she wears a warm, comforting smile. Kindergarten teachers *expect* things to happen. They *plan* for things to happen. They plan how they will *respond* when things happen. And they have the *tools* they need in order to respond the best way they can.

As a group, we teachers are skilled in planning. We think things through. We map out our days. We have our supplies and materials ready. We question ourselves: If I teach this, how might students respond? We anticipate what might happen on any given day. We like to be prepared, because we know day-to-day teaching is enormously complex. Preparation helps us feel empowered, informed; it strengthens our teaching and our responses to our students. It is also a big part of success in small-group work.

Planning for small-group conferences might at first seem a contradiction in terms. After all, we can't be sure what our students will do on any given day in response to our teaching, can we? No, we can't. But we can take a good guess, just like the kindergarten teacher who can't be sure who her fresh crop of new faces will be and how they will respond to her and the new environment. She anticipates predictable problems and plans her responses to those problems by relying on what she knows from last year and the year before that and the one before that. She relies on what she knows about kindergartners. She relies on what she knows about the parents of kindergartners, especially first-timers. And she meets regularly with other kindergarten teachers to share ideas: "This happened once and here's what I did. What works for me is. . . ."

We can plan our units of study—the big goals and possible teaching points that fit around them—and our small-group instruction in the same way: by taking a good guess. And our guesses get better and better when we meet regularly with our colleagues. When planning small-group work, what really matters is anticipating possibilities and problems. If we take really good guesses and talk them over with our colleagues, we'll be prepared for whatever comes. And come it will!

Teachers often meet as grade-level teams to plan an upcoming writing unit of study. Many find it helpful to lay minilesson ideas out on a calendar (see Figure 2.1).

After laying that foundation, there are four ways to plan potential small-group instruction: studying qualities of good writing, studying whole-class minilessons, setting goals for classroom expectations, and establishing bottom lines.

Potential Small-Group Teaching Based on Qualities of Good Writing

Qualities of good writing—topic choice/idea, elaboration/details, voice, focus, organization/structure, conventions, spelling—span all genres. We can take a list of the qualities of good writing and think, *What are some ways I can remind students of these in this particular unit?* Studying the qualities of good writing is especially helpful when planning table conferences (see Chapter 6).

Unit 6: Exploring Poetry
Writing

Feb 1-28   **CFL-SAI Unit Planning Calendar**

"Hidden Poem" Book Basket

How to see the world like a poet Copies of poems	How to write observations like a poet not a scientist *give leaf not safety pin*	How to find the places where poetry hides *wonder door* share - observation door	Heart Door	How to write w/ line break
Read your poem out loud and listen to the sound	Show a strong a feeling by showing not telling	Use your senses to describe anything	↓ more practice	How to write w/ the voice of poetry speak to subject
Write with exact words	How to Recognize and Use patterns in poems	How to write with a simile (comparisons)	✓ compare a story w/ + w/out a simile	How to take a story and Revise it into a story poem
		(2 days) ← Frames - Decorate	clean up poem for publication Practice reading	Celebration coffee house invite parents

Valentines - do senses poem - love

Figure 2.1   First-Grade Poetry Calendar

Figure 2.2 lists a number of potential teaching points related to the qualities of good writing.

Potential Small-Group Teaching Based on Whole-Class Minilessons

After I've thought about what I'll teach in a unit of study and in what order, I study each minilesson. If I teach this minilesson to the whole class, how will it affect their independent writing and my conferences? What if kids try the strategy or technique I have taught and they struggle? How will I respond? What about the students who apply the writing technique or strategy with

Qualities of Good Writing	Potential Teaching Points (Possible Table Conferences)
• Choosing appropriate topics/ideas	• Writers make time lines of the last few days. • Writers often think of a big strong feeling and times we've felt that way. • Writers consider important people, places, or things and think, *What's happened lately when I've been with that person?*
• Using sketches to prompt details	• Writers sketch the important parts of stories: setting (Where was I exactly?), character (Who was there?), action (What was I doing with my body?). • Writers add speech bubbles to the sketch by asking, "Who said what?" • Writers add thought shots to the sketch by asking, "What was I thinking?" • Writers ask, "What was I feeling?" and add expression to the character's face.
• Elaborating/adding details (add internal thinking, dialogue, small action, setting details, buddy sentences, descriptive sentences, facts, anecdotes, examples)	• Writers elaborate by studying the sketch and writing all the details of the sketch (setting details, action details . . .). • Writers elaborate the big important part of the story by telling that part in tiny little steps. • Writers don't elaborate by writing all action, action, action. Mix it up! Action. Dialogue. Action. Thought shot.
• Creating organization/structure (beginning, middle, end; table of contents; headings/subheadings)	• Writers orally tell their story across their fingers before writing anything on the page. • Writers touch each page, thinking, *What happened first, and then, and then?* • Writers use a time line to plan how their stories will go. • Writers often think, *What's the big thing that happens in my story?* and lots of times they put that part in the middle.
• Creating a distinctive voice	• Writers use the "mom" technique to add voice, asking themselves, "Would my mom recognize that it's me telling the story?" • Writers pay attention to phrases and interjections (Yowza! Cool! Awesome!) commonly used in speech and add those to our writing. • Writers use punctuation to bring out our voice in our writing.

Figure 2.2 Potential Table Conferences (*continues*)

Figure 2.2 (*continued*)

• Maintaining focus (small moment, one idea, one event)	• Writers ask, "What's this story about? What do I want my reader to learn/understand? What is the heart of the story?"
	• Writers often ask, "What's the big thing here?" and make sure all parts of the story have to do with the big thing.
	• Writers often ask, "Am I telling about my whole day or I am telling about one small part of my day?" We try to zoom in on a moment and tell it in detail.
• Making revisions	• Writers often show, not tell their feelings.
	• Writers understand that revision isn't just adding in but also taking out.
	• Writers use the "magic of three" to create rhythm in the language.
	• Reread piece out loud: Does it make sense? Does it sound right?
	• Writers pay special attention to verbs, asking, "Is this exactly what I want my reader to picture?"
• Following conventions (capitalization, end punctuation)	• Writers use end punctuation (not just when editing, but always) so the reader knows exactly how to read the piece.
	• Writers capitalize the beginning of each new sentence as well as proper nouns.
• Using correct spelling (frequently used words, genre-related words)	• Writers reread, asking, "Is this a word-wall word?" and make corrections.
	• Writers notice familiar word patterns to spell words correctly.

great success? Can I stretch them further as writers? It helps a great deal for me to write my thoughts down.

Anticipating students' responses to our teaching is especially helpful when planning potential skill conferences (see Chapter 7). We cannot be sure of these responses until we teach the lessons, but we can take good guesses, especially in the company of colleagues, and be ready for most of what may happen. Figure 2.3 lists a number of teaching points related to whole-class minilessons.

Unit Minilessons (First-Grade Poetry)	Potential Teaching Points (Possible Skill Conferences)
Poets come up with ideas by opening the doors of poetry.	*Can't think of any poem ideas*: Tell them you think about places you love to go, and then make a poem about the things you do in that place.
	Has tons of ideas, writing poem after poem after poem: Mention that poets linger on one poem, adding details (elaborating) before moving on.
Poets use line breaks to create rhythm and music.	*Poem looks like a story (no line breaks)*: Either fold writing paper in half or provide half-sheets as a reminder of what poems often look like.
	Line breaks appear anywhere on the page: Show an example of a poem with line breaks, studying where and why the poet used them.
Poets use repetition to create rhythm and music.	*Poets use repetition, but the words or lines repeated seem insignificant*: Show an example of a poem with a repeating line and study where and why the writer decided to repeat those words.
	Poets have evidence of a repeating line: Teach the poets how to establish a pattern using a repeating line and then give the pattern a twist ("Things" by Eloise Greenfield [1978] is a good example of this technique).
Poets show, not tell their feelings.	*Poets tell their feelings*: Demonstrate the way you circle a feeling in your poem, and show that feeling by telling three small actions (love = I wrapped my arms around Granny. My heart went thumpity thump. And I didn't let go).
	Poets show their feelings: Poets often use repetition to show a big strong feeling: I wrapped my arms around Granny My heart went thumpity thump And I didn't let go. No I didn't let go.
Poets make comparisons to help readers make pictures in their minds.	*Comparisons are too closely related (his smile was like a huge grin)*: Teach the group that poets often compare something concrete (something you can hold in your hands or touch) to something abstract (an idea or feeling/cannot hold it in your hands): His smile was like a wish come true *or* that poets compare by using a shape: His smile was the shape of a watermelon slice. *or* Compare by using the weather: His smile was like the warm sunshine.
	Poets make comparisons using similes: Teach the students another way poets make comparisons, called *metaphors*. One way to do this is to take away the words, *is like a* or *was like a* and replace them with the words *is a* or *was a* like this . . . His smile was like the warm sunshine. His smile was the warm sunshine.

Figure 2.3   Potential Skill Conferences (*continues*)

Figure 2.3 *(continued)*

Poets write even longer and longer poems.	*Poets write short poems*: Teach the group that one way writers write even longer poems is to sketch and add details from the sketch to the poem.
	Poets write longer poems: Show the students how poets often group three or four lines that go together, called *stanzas*, leave white space, and group another three or four lines that go together.

Potential Small-Group Teaching Based on Classroom Expectations

In my district, we spend a lot of time early in the year establishing and reinforcing our expectations regarding writing workshop. Our first unit of study might have a title like Launching the Writing Workshop: The Conditions Necessary for a Successful Year. It is chock-full of whole-class minilessons: how our writing workshop goes; what we writers do when we think we are done; how to be a perfect partner; how to keep our writing folders neat and tidy—the list goes on and on. After we've taught these expectation minilessons early and listed general expectations and behavior on a chart, we spend the rest of the year focusing mostly on content minilessons. This serves most students' needs just fine.

Some students, though, need more. If most students in the class do, we include classroom-expectation minilessons in each subsequent unit of study. The majority of the time, though, only a handful of students in a class need reminding, and then small-group instruction is the perfect way to handle it. Figure 2.4 lists a number of potential teaching points related to classroom expectations and behavior.

Potential Small-Group Teaching Based on the Bottom Line

Students in our classrooms are extremely diverse. We celebrate that diversity, of course. We expect that when we teach X, students will go off and do X, Y, and Z (and some will do U, V, and W). Yet we hold high expectations for *all* our students. So when I say *bottom-line standards,* I certainly don't mean *bottom of the barrel.* Rather, I mean, what are the three or four essential goals of this unit? (These are usually easily determined from district and/or state standards.)

We will probably teach between fifteen and twenty-five minilessons in a monthlong unit. It's wise, therefore, to figure out the bottom lines or big goals for the unit, check students' progress, and teach and reteach these essential skills to small groups of students as necessary.

One way to reteach an essential skill is to change the teaching tool. For example, if a bottom-line standard is for all of our students to be able to show, not tell their feelings, we could first demonstrate with an example from our own writing. Next, we could point out additional examples in published

Expectations/Behavior	Potential Teaching Points (Possible Expectation Conferences)
Independence	• Let me remind you how writers have materials ready. • I want to teach you how to solve your own problems. • I decide who I confer with, but I promise to meet with you at least once a week.
Productivity	• We writers pay attention not just to what we're writing but also to how much we are writing. • Writers set goals each day, each week.
Focus (staying on task)	• Sometimes if I am having difficulty staying focused on my writing, I stop, take a deep breath, try to picture my topic/idea in my head, and go back to my writing. • Noises easily distract me, too; whenever this happens to me, I. . . .
Organization (of materials)	• Watch me look through my writing folder in order to find what I am looking for. Notice I have my drafts on this side. . . . • Let me show you what I do when I finish with my folder. You can do this, too!
Responsibility (taking folders and pieces of writing home and bringing them back)	• Often I keep a to-do list reminding me of the important things I need to do each day. Isn't that smart? Keep this list with you, always reminding you of the things you need to carry to and from school each day.
Approach to writing (eager? drags feet?)	• I want to teach you that writers don't waste a single moment of their writing time. . . . • Today, let's study our calendars, noticing especially our date for publication and celebration so we can set goals for our writing.

Figure 2.4 Potential Expectation Conferences

Bottom-Line Standards	Potential Teaching Points (Possible Progress Conferences)
Choosing an interesting topic you know about	• Who are some people, places, or things you know a lot about? • Try out several topics to see whether they are good fits. • Think about who will read your piece—your audience—and what they will want to read about.
Spelling words correctly	• Whenever you're writing, check the word wall to help you spell those words. • Writers use known word-wall words to spell unknown words (if I can spell *house*, I can spell *blouse*). • When you're finished writing, go back and reread, checking words on the word wall.
Sticking with one topic over several pages, telling more and more and more about that one topic	• Writers ask themselves, "What's the big thing (action/feeling) my story is about?" They sketch the big thing on each page. • Writers add words to show what's happening and they make sure the words tell about the "big thing." • Writers revise by stretching out the "heart" part of their story (the part that reveals the big emotion or action), telling more and more about not just what happened but their reaction to what happened.
Writing at least three sentences on each page	• Writers set goals for themselves, writing more and more each day. • Writers go back and reread their piece, asking, "Did I meet my goal?" • Writers write different kinds of sentences (action, thought, action *or* setting, action, dialogue).

Figure 2.5 Potential Progress Conferences

books or in other students' pieces. The teaching doesn't change; the vehicle does. It's also helpful to plan a series of small-group conferences on a bottom-line standard, each conference building on the next (progress conferences, see Chapter 9). Figure 2.5 is a list of potential teaching points related to bottom-line standards.

Planning small-group work based on predictable classroom responses to the ideas presented in Figures 2.2–2.5 is an essential way not only to be prepared to meet the needs of our students as they are challenged by new material, but also to provide continual small-group support of the consistent hard work we expect from our students in writers' workshop throughout the year.

Forming Groups on the Basis of Assessment

Once you have planned some of the potential teaching points for meeting with small groups of children in conferences (Chapter 2), you'll want to test some of those theories out. Will the students in your classroom do any of the things you and your colleagues anticipated they would? Of course they will. *But how will you go about finding out?*

There are many ways to assess students as writers: by observing them at work, by talking with them about their writing, and by reading their work. When we assess our students with the idea of forming small groups, we want to look for patterns of behavior, patterns of need, and patterns of strength.

Wider assessment is a necessary part of working with small groups in the writing workshop. We teach our minilessons and we send our students off to write independently. As they are writing, we assess the *class* in order to obtain information to help these students become better writers. We evaluate the content of the pieces (genre, topic, structure, focus, elaboration, voice, syntax, conventions, spelling) and the students' writing process skills. We also observe the behavior and attitudes our students hold and demonstrate (independence, stamina, rigor, ability to work cooperatively).

When we assess our entire class, we usually do so with a particular goal or goals in mind. Carl Anderson (2005) refers to this as creating a "lens through which we can look at student writers." In order to help us form small groups, we can research the room and collect student work.

Researching the Room

Rather than immediately working with one child, I spend the first five minutes reading over students' shoulders, quickly noting what these writers are attempting. I ask, "How's it going?" or "What are you working on?" take a few notes, and move on. I look for patterns that will help me decide future teaching points for small-group and individual work. Noticing that a child who is trying to add dialogue could benefit from my help, I think, *Are there any other children in the room who could benefit from this same strategy right now?* Most often, the answer to that question is yes.

Why five minutes? Because it's both long enough and short enough. I can effectively research the work of ten or fifteen students in five minutes. I move from child to child very quickly. Often I'm looking for something specific and predetermined. If I don't find what I'm looking for, I might stop and ask a few probing questions and study the writing a little more closely. One of those moments might go something like this:

"How's it going, Nazir?"

"I'm writing my story."

"Is this the story you're writing about the train ride with your mom?" I quickly read what he's written so far and offer an affirmation: "Thanks, Nazir. Wow! You are working hard to get your details down. Keep going!"

Spending ten or fifteen minutes researching the room would throw my work in the classroom off balance. In those extra five or ten minutes, I can hold two or three individual or group conferences. Our students need to benefit from our time. They should be seeing us more often, not less often.

However, my research is neither cold nor sterile. I touch students' shoulders or give them a thumbs-up. I respond with a smile, a gesture, or a quick compliment—some affirmation that the child is doing good work. I always remember that these are children I am working with, children telling the personal stories of their lives on the page. My intention, whether moving about the room or having a one-to-one conversation, is to leave every child I talk to feeling uplifted by a sense of accomplishment.

Research Through a Teaching Point Lens

One way to research the room is in relation to the teaching point of the day's minilesson. I write my teaching point on a piece of paper and make three columns:

Who in this class is doing this now?	Who in this class is almost doing this now?	Who in the class is *not* doing this now?

Who in this class is doing this now? In *On Common Ground* (2005), DuFour and his coauthors suggest that teachers, in conjunction with their colleagues, answer three crucial questions:

- What do we want each student to learn?
- How will we know when each student has learned it?
- How will we respond when a student experiences difficulty in learning?

I would add a crucial fourth question to that list:

- How will we respond when students experience success?

Recently I accompanied a handful of principals from my district to a fourth-grade classroom where we observed a writing workshop in action. We watched as master teacher Barrie Evans taught her students how writers sometimes lead with a description of the setting, which she labeled a "picture-perfect lead." After the minilesson, the students wrote at their tables while Barrie circulated. At one point she gathered a few students together on the carpeted area and taught them how to add a simile to their picture-perfect lead.

Later we discussed our visit. What struck the principals most was that Barrie met with the students who were applying the minilesson *successfully* and helped them move forward. "Many teachers would have left those students alone, and that's a problem," a principal commented.

In one area of our district, a good majority of the students begin the year already meeting or exceeding grade-level expectations. The regional supervisor of those schools posed a challenge to her principals: "A year's worth of gains for *every* child." Their mission was established and clear. That day, Barrie showed them a method for achieving that mission.

Because there are students in *any* classroom who meet and exceed expectations, we need to know which students are doing what things really well so we can teach them strategies to become even better writers.

Who in this class is almost doing this now? Students who are "almost doing this now" are making an attempt to put into practice whatever we've taught that day but clearly need more help. Often our children have the *what* but lack the *how*. For example, Mrs. Casey taught her second graders how to add end punctuation to help the reader know how to read the piece. After the minilesson, as she read over students' shoulders, she noticed a few children were adding periods at the end of every line instead of at the end of each thought. They were giving the teaching point a try—they understood the *what,* adding end punctuation—but lacked the *how.* Because using proper end punctuation is one of the bottom-line standards or main goals of the unit, Mrs. Casey met with these students in a small group to help them add end punctuation properly. Then she checked their progress again and again until they were able to apply the skill independently.

In our research, we look for the errors our students are making while attempting new strategies, and we help small groups of students who are making similar errors.

Who in the class is not *doing this now?* Asking this question can give us valuable information. Other times, it may not tell us anything at all.

When we teach a minilesson, we don't necessarily expect that every child will go off and try out that skill or strategy that day. Rather, we expect that everyone will add the strategy to her or his growing repertoire of strategies and apply the skill when it is appropriate. So it's possible that the children who are "not doing this now" just don't need to try it out now. And that's okay.

There are times, however, when we want all the students to apply a particular skill or strategy immediately. In this case, I incorporate an "assignment" when I send them off to work independently. For example, "Today, when you go back to your seats, I'd like all of us to practice revising a story. For today, let's not start any new stories. Writers, will you please choose a story you've already written, reread it, and ask yourselves, 'Is this a story I care about deeply and perhaps have more to say about?' Because as writers we revise stories we care deeply about and want to work on some more to make them even better!"

When we record student names in the "not doing this now" column, we need to ask ourselves:

- Are the same names appearing over and over again?
- Was the teaching point a strategy for anytime we write (as most are)?
- Was the strategy assigned to the class?
- Is this a strategy within the child's grasp?

The answers to these questions inform our decisions about when and whether to gather these students together in a small group.

Research Through a Goals Lens

We can also research the room with several teaching points in mind. Chapter 2 discusses how to focus on a few goals by establishing some bottom lines for the unit. Those same bottom lines help us decide what to focus on when we research the room. An especially helpful tool is to take the three or four goals we want to hone in on and jot them down. Then, while we're doing our initial five minutes of research, we can look for these specific things and jot down students' names using a three-tiered criteria: strong evidence (+), some evidence (√), very little to no evidence (0). The resulting student clusters are possible small groups. (See the example in Figure 3.1.)

Another way to research the room with goals in mind is to prepare a form listing the students' names and the big goals of the unit, create a rubric establishing degrees of success in meeting those goals (see Figure 3.2), and enter the rubric codes on the chart. The completed chart (see Figure 3.3) is a snapshot of the class that can be examined for patterns. Are there clusters of students who could benefit from instruction in a skill? Are there clusters of children who could benefit from extending the skill? We can then form small groups based on those patterns.

Research Through a Writing Process Lens

When researching the writing process, we have two questions in mind:

- Where are the students in the process?
- How can we help them along in that process?

Writing Goals/ Bottom-Line Standards	Assessing Students for Potential Small Groups		
Students read several feature articles and notice how the writer organized the piece, figure out the angle or focus, and notice specific strategies for elaborating ideas or paragraphs.	+	Brian, Rebecca, Mariah, Madison	
	√	Jose, Tamara, Nash	
	0	Giselle	
Students choose a topic that reflects a specific interest, a personal connection, or a hobby and find an interesting angle from which to approach it.	+	Brian, Rebecca, Jose, Mariah, Madison	
	√	Tony, Giselle	
	0	Connie	
Students elaborate using a variety of strategies: research, direct quotes, interviews, small actions, physical description, material weighted according to its importance.	+	Rebecca, Jose, Tamara, Noah	
	√	Brian, Connie, Tony, Giselle	
	0		
Students use appropriate punctuation, especially for direct quotes.	+	Brian, Jose, Nash, Noah	
	√	Giselle, Alex, Mariah, Madison	
	0	Tony	

Figure 3.1   Assessing for Small Groups: Bottom Line Standards

We can determine pretty quickly where our students are in the process of writing by watching them write and paying attention to what they are writing. For example, if students in upper-grade classrooms are writing in notebooks, they are most likely prewriting or rehearsing a draft. If they are writing on legal pads, they are drafting and/or revising. If the piece is messy with carets, scratch-outs, and extra paper taped or stapled to the draft pad, they are obviously knee-deep in revision.

In the primary grades, students often write one story (or draft) after another after another. They finish one and start a new one. In a quick look around the room, we notice the paper kids are choosing. Are some choosing new paper? If so, we can form a small group of these students and teach a strategy writers use when starting a new story. Are some continuing to work on a story in progress? We can teach those students a strategy writers use to remember stories and continue working on those stories. Are other students working on multipage stories? If so, we can form groups according to how far along they are, teaching/reteaching strategies writers use to write the beginning of a story, stretch out the middle of their story, or end their story.

Unit 1	# of +⊕=	Sketch c/a/s	labels	Stretching out wds	Across 3 pages	Sketch matches writing
1 Sabrene	1	⊕ + ⊕	+			
2 Lelilani	25	⊕ + ⊕	+	⊕	⊕	⊕
3 Brandon	3	+ C − −	−	−	−	−
4 Rachel	11	+ − +	−	+	+ title pg	+
Juan						
~~Keyshawn~~						
5 Nicole	8	⊕ + ⊕	+	+	⊕	⊕
6 Sarah	6	⊕ + ⊕	−	+ mid sounds	+	⊕
7 Alicia	8	⊕ − +	−	−	−	−
8 Penelope	2	⊕⊕ ⊕	+	⊕	⊕	⊕
9 J'Dakis	16	− − −	−	−	−	−
10 Saverio	3	+ − +	−	−	+ Sketch	−
11 Courtney	9	⊕ − +	+	− random stg	⊕	−
12 Robert	7	⊕ + ⊕	+	+	+ the end	+
13 Jason	3	⊕ + ⊕	⊕	⊕	⊕	+
14 Daniel	5	⊕ + ⊕	−	⊕	⊕	⊕
Gabriel	9	⊕ + +	−	+	⊕	⊕
15 Ashlyne	6	⊕ + ⊕	+	⊕	⊕	⊕
16 Reece	7	⊕ + ⊕	+	⊕	⊕	⊕
17 Jonathon	15 no words	+ − −	−	−	−	−

Figure 3.2   Rubric

	Increase Stamina	Be in the Moment	Build Tension	Show, Not Tell
Dennardra	+	0	0	0
Jozelle	+	+	√	+
Nicholas	√	√	√	√
Payne	+	+	√	0
Miles	+	√	0	√
Jake	√	√	√	+
Amber	+	√	√	+

Figure 3.3   Assessing for Small Groups: A Classroom Snapshot

Jennifer McCafferty teaches her students to monitor their own writing process. In her classroom, she hangs a series of paper plates, each plate labeled with a step of the writing process: prewriting, drafting, revising, editing, and publishing. There are also as many clothes pins as there are students in the class, each one labeled with a student's name. When Jennifer launches a unit, all the clothes pins are attached to the "prewriting" plate. As her students cycle independently through the process, they move their assigned arrow from plate to plate, giving Jennifer a quick snapshot of which students are in which step. (See Figure 3.4.) If she sees that Steven, Crystal, Shadonna, and Ryleigh are all revising, she can gather them as a group and teach or reteach a revision technique or skill.

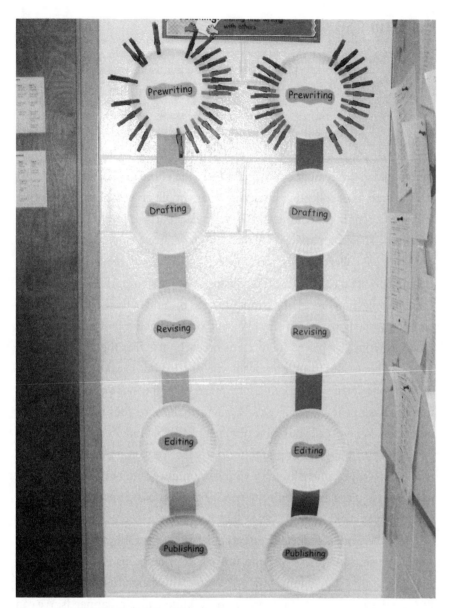

Figure 3.4 Students Monitor Their Own Writing Process

Collecting Student Work

If we use student work to plan future teaching points for small-group instruction, the work is best collected at the beginning and in the middle of a unit rather than at the end (when work is traditionally collected). We can then study this work, asking "What am I noticing about this piece of writing? Is this true for others in my class?" If we do this work in conjunction with our colleagues, we can widen the comparison population to the entire grade level.

The process of collecting work can be as simple or as sophisticated as we make it, depending on our lens. We can collect parts or pieces of work, with something specific in mind, or we can collect complete stories/drafts.

When we collect specific student work, it is usually related to the day's teaching point or a big goal of the unit and is either an example of the point or goal or a reflection on it. For example, toward the end of the write-and-confer part of a workshop, I might say, "Writers, we have about four minutes left in which to write. I've placed index cards on each table. For the next four minutes, will you read through the leads you've tried out in your notebook and copy the one you are considering for your story on the index card?" After four minutes have gone by, I then say, "Writers, make sure your name is on your index card. When I call your table number, place your index card in the basket on the way to the gathering area for our share session." (An alternative to recopying—especially helpful for younger writers—is to have students hand in the whole piece so far with the specific portion of interest marked with a sticky note or sticky arrow.)

Once the work is collected, we can then sort it according to our needs. We can create separate piles—Who in this class is doing this now (+)? Who in this class is almost doing this now ($\sqrt{}$)? Who in this class is not doing this now (0)?—and use the piles to form groups of children with similar needs. We can also score the work (4, 3, 2, 1) and separate it into piles that way. This method "grades" the writing in addition to helping us form small groups. (In order for us to grade the work, it must pertain to something we expect all children to have done.)

When evaluating work in relation to the big goals of the unit, we can use the same sort of rubric presented in Figure 3.2. The patterns that emerge

| Student Name | Studying the Volume | Studying the Sketches | | | | Studying the Words | | | | | |
	Volume (# of lines)	Character	Action	Setting	Labels	Character Action	Dialogue	Internal Thinking	Feelings	Setting Details	Conventions of Print
Kyla	16	+	+	+	0	+	√	√	+	√	+
Reiker	17	+	+	+	+	√	√	0	√	√	√
Maggie	18	+	+	+	0	√	√	√	0	√	+
Van	15	+	+	+	0	+	√	√	√	0	√
Lesley	19	+	+	+	0	+	0	0	√	√	+

Figure 3.5 Assessing Student Work for Patterns to Form Small Groups

will help us determine small groups and the teaching points for those groups.

Recently, a second-grade teacher I was working with created a form on which she was able to capture her assessment of her students' volume of writing (number of lines), the sketches they drew, and the words they wrote, all in relation to the goals her school's second-grade team had established for their narrative unit (see Figure 3.5). Notice how the information in each column helps her form small groups for specific instruction. For example, the teaching point "How writers add dialogue to stories" would benefit a group made up of Kyla, Reiker, Maggie, and Van.

Small Groups Needn't Always Be Made Up of Students with Like Needs

In a third-grade classroom recently, I witnessed the power of forming a group of students with heterogeneous needs. The class was studying Vera B. Williams' *A Chair for My Mother* (1982). The teacher pointed out how Vera set up the story by including a lot of "background information" in the lead. A few kids in the class were struggling to understand the concept of "background information" and apply it in their own writing. However, Julian cruised right along, explaining that he was telling "specific stuff" about what had happened to his brother and him before the basketball game. The teacher wisely put Julian in a group with the children who were having a hard time. She retaught the strategy using Julian's words, Julian's added input, and Julian's piece: "Writers, do you see how Julian is telling 'specific stuff' about what happened before, just like Vera did in her story?" The result was amazing. Lightbulbs turned on. Because Julian's language made sense to them, the group was inspired to apply the writing strategy with more success.

As you've seen, there are many ways to assess students in order to form small groups, whether on the spot while students are writing or later by looking at work you have collected. No method is better than another. The important thing is to find the approach that works best for you. My guess is it will be a mixture of both process and product.

Gathering
Teaching Tools

One day some time ago, I was working with Ms. Bookman, a teacher new to trying out small-group work in the writing workshop. Her first graders were in the first week of a poetry unit. Her teaching point was, Poets often get their ideas from big strong feelings they have in their hearts. After the minilesson, the children went to their tables and began to write. Ms. Bookman and I researched the room for about five minutes.

One of the big goals Ms. Bookman set for the class was that their poems "looked and sounded like poems." As we circulated, we noticed that a few students had written poems that looked and sounded like small-moment stories (the kind of writing they had been doing earlier in the year). Ms. Bookman tapped each of these students quietly on the shoulder and asked her or him to come to a corner of the rug. When everyone had gathered, Ms. Bookman complimented the students, telling them she had noticed how they hadn't just sat down and started a new poem but instead had reread yesterday's work and continued working on that poem. Then she told them she had also noticed that their poems looked a lot like the stories they were used to writing. And then she stopped. Her eyes grew large and she looked at me with a hint of panic—*I've got them together, now what?*

In order to help small groups of students with some aspect of their writing, I need to be prepared. One way I do that is to carry a notebook with me while I confer. In Roy Peter Clark's *Writing Tools: 50 Essential Strategies for Every Writer* (2006), he describes fifty tools every writer needs. Tool 44 is "Save string. *For big projects, save scraps others would toss.*" Mr. Clark explains, "To save string, I need a simple file box. . . . As soon as I declare my interest in an important topic, a number of things happen. I notice more things about my topic. Then I have conversations about it with friends and colleagues. They feed my interest. One by one, my box fills with items" (214).

I fill my conferring notebook in much the same way. Whenever I write, read, talk with colleagues, and attend professional development seminars and come across interesting material I can use to teach students, *I save string*. I organize these ideas in a appropriate section of my conferring notebook (a three-ring binder): my own writing (notebook entries, drafts, published pieces); various kinds of paper; student writing; mentor or exemplar texts; and a resource section with strategy charts and advice from published writers. I prefer the three-ring binders with pockets. That way I can tuck books I am using as mentor texts there.

These are the *teaching tools* I carry with me as I confer with small groups of students. They help me demonstrate or explain writing strategies to my students.

My Own Writing

I save a lot of the writing I do in class and some of the writing I do elsewhere. I file it away in my folders and notebooks, because I know I will use it again when I'm conducting small-group conferences. I have many samples, in many genres, on different kinds of paper—drafts, published work, and everything in between. I have one-page stories, three-page stories, stories with sketches, stories without, how-to books, poems, all-about books, expository essays, literary essays, feature articles . . . the list goes on and on. (I bring a composition book to upper-grade classrooms, because that's what the kids usually write in.)

When I write in preparation for teaching, I do so with great purpose and expectation. If I expect that some of my students will write "summary" stories rather than "in-the-moment" stories, then I want summary stories as well as in-the-moment stories in my notebook. I can then use my own writing to teach a group of students a strategy I use as a writer to recognize I am writing summaries and then how I write "in the moment" instead.

I didn't always do this. I used to write pieces in hopes that I would dazzle my students with what it means to be a writer: what good writing looks like, sounds like, feels like. My moment of enlightenment occurred during a summer writing institute at Columbia Teachers College. Emily Smith, our section leader, suggested that we could think about our writer's notebook in much more ambitious ways: that we set them up in a planned and meaningful way, generating the kinds of lists, entries, and prewriting work we anticipate our students may do. Our writing notebooks should be a teaching tool designed for classroom use.

So now, in the personal narrative section of one of my notebooks that I use with upper grades, you'll find:

- lists of story ideas
- entry after entry (some with the date/some without)
- entries written in the moment
- entries written as summaries
- entries I could care less about
- entries I care about deeply—some in which I'll surely want to invest more time
- time lines
- several different leads for the same story

Figure 4.1 shows a few pages from one of those notebooks.

My colleague Gail Ramsdell, a kindergarten staff developer, shared a helpful strategy with me that I have used over and over: make several copies of your drafts. That way you can use the same teaching text again and again to get at different strategies in your small-group conferences.

Various Kinds of Paper

Primary writing teachers know the importance of different kinds of paper. Their writing supply areas are full of choices. They know it is imperative that students use paper that matches their writing development. Primary teachers know when students need just a single page, when to add more lines for writing and decrease the size of the box for the drawing, and when to add more pages. Upper-grade teachers also realize the value of the type of

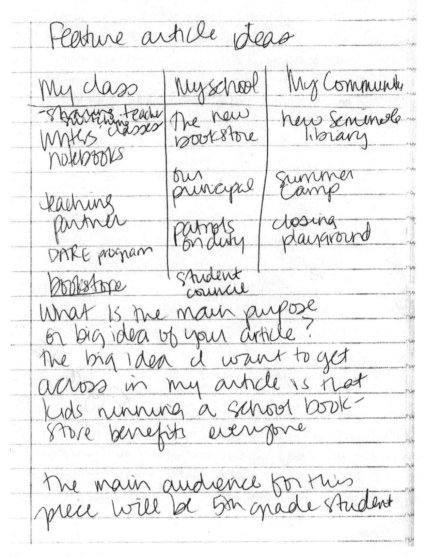

Figure 4.1a Notebook Entry: Generating Ideas for a Feature Article

paper. Whether students struggle or experience great success when writing, the paper they use can provide a framework or structure that supports and deepens the writing. We are wise to keep several kinds of paper choices at the ready in our conferring folder.

For example, when planning a unit of study on poetry, it is strategic to think:

Another reason I like to go to the beach when the weather gets hot is cooling off in the ~~so damp sub~~

~~top~~
The white sand can be hot, but if you dig down deep the sand underneath is wet and cool.

The ~~wet an~~ farther you dig, the harder and cooler the sand ~~gets~~

One summer day, my daughter Ella was really hot at the beach. We dug a huge hole and started ~~packing~~ spreading cool wet handfuls of sand all over her body. I was thinking "Gross" but Ella said, "Mom this sand is so cool!"

Figure 4.1b   Notebook Entry: Elaborating an Essay Paragraph Using a "Hanger"

If I see . . .	*I might . . .*
children writing poems that look like stories	provide paper with short lines to encourage line breaks
children writing sophisticated and lengthy free verse	provide poetry paper with white space between the stanzas

11-12

people: Tim
→ picked up wiggly roach
→ ride her bike without training
→ burnt the chicken

One day I picked up dead roach off the living room kitchen floor. Only it wasn't dead! It wiggled when I picked it up. I dropped it and screamed, "TIM!" Tim ran in the kitchen & picked up the roach.

On Saturday Tim tried to teach Ella how to ride her bike without training wheels. After a few times across the field he said, "Forget it!" Then I tried to do the same. After a few tries, I said, "forget it!"

Figure 4.1c   Notebook Entry: Generating Entries Off of a List

Strategy Charts

Often in a minilesson, we teach a strategy—a series of steps—that will help students learn, practice, and apply a particular writing skill or technique. Many teachers create a chart listing these steps and hang it on a wall in the classroom, so students can look at it for support when they are writing on their own.

Of course, not all our charts can fit on the classroom walls. And even if we do manage to display a ton of writing strategy charts, we eventually have to take some of them down to make way for new charts and new units of study. Therefore, I list the strategy steps in my notebook. When I need to, I can pull a group of students together, remind them about the strategy, and show them the steps.

Student Writing

Student work can also serve as models and examples. Whenever I am working in classrooms and encounter examples of good writing, I photocopy them to use as teaching tools. I attach a sticky note stating why I copied the work so I'll remember and can grab the right example when I need it.

Students are inspired by work produced by their peers. If I am conferring with a small group of students in a first grade all-about unit, I love to pull out an all-about book written by another first grader. The message is clear: You can do this, too! Many teachers use the same pieces for years.

Just yesterday my daughter, a first grader, sat down next to me and wrote this poem:

> I love to
> play because
> playing is ful
> of acshin
> runing walking
> playing hide in seek
> tag
> jump ropeing
> jumping

When she finished, she read it to me with pride, and I responded as any parent would: "I love your poem!" And as soon as Ella left the room, the writing teacher in me grabbed her poem and placed it in my writing crate. I love the rhythm she created by using repetition. I love the way she set up a pattern by repeating the *ing* words and also how she broke the pattern with *tag* and made it a line on its own. Did Ella write her poem with those intentions in mind? No. However, I can teach a small group of students to use patterns and repetition in their poems *as if she did*.

Mentor or Exemplar Texts

The first-grade team at Rawlings Elementary, in St. Petersburg, Florida, gathered to plan an author study on Ezra Jack Keats. They chose *Peter's Chair* and *A Letter to Amy* as texts they wanted to read aloud and study—specifically what Ezra has done as a writer that they imagine their first-grade students trying out in their own writing.

They also studied student work from the previous unit on personal narratives and noticed that although most of the students were writing stories several pages long, many of them wrote only one sentence on each page. They decided one of the big goals for the author study would be: Writers elaborate to bring the detail of the story to the reader.

After they had determined all the big goals for the unit, as well as some possible teaching points, they used sticky notes to mark parts of the stories they could highlight in minilessons. Next, they thought about the struggles and successes their students might have. They used different-colored sticky notes to mark pages in the stories they might use as scaffolds in small groups.

Finally, they predicted the responses of the students—they took a good guess. With regard to the detail goal, they decided that some of the students would continue to write only one sentence per page. They also decided that some students (especially those already writing more than one sentence on a page) would need a stronger push toward more sophisticated writing. To that end, they planned a possible minilesson and two small-group conferences using the story *Peter's Chair*.

Whole-class minilesson: Writers elaborate—writing more and more on each page to bring the detail of the story to the reader
Strategy: Ask, what happened? Who said what?

Examples from book:

> Peter looked in Susie's room . . .
>
> "Hi, Peter," said his father . . .

Small-group conference for students who need *this strategy:* Writers elaborate by adding a buddy sentence on each page

Small-group conference for students who already use the strategy: Writers not only elaborate by writing more and more on each page but also by adding pages to the middle of their story

Examples from book:

> They went outside and stood in front of his house . . .
>
> But he couldn't fit . . .
>
> His mother came . . .

Advice from Published Writers

When I read advice from writers or read books about writing well, I have two purposes. The first is, How does what I'm reading influence my writing? The second is, How could what I'm reading be shared with children to influence them as writers?

In my conferring notebook, I carry an interview with the writer Janet Fitch that was published in *Oprah* magazine. In it, Janet Fitch reveals her daily routine of writing: how she gets up, takes the kids to school, makes coffee, and sit downs and writes for hours, every day. Many times I have pulled that interview from my notebook and showed it to a small group of students who needed help understanding the daily writing routine, building stamina, or setting goals.

Another indispensable teaching tool I carry with me wherever I go, but especially when conferring, is *Writing Tools: 50 Essential Strategies for Every Writer,* by Roy Peter Clark (2006). I love this book for the practical advice he offers to writers, young and old. And I love this book because I don't know everything there is to know about the teaching of writing. Lots of times I assess the needs of a group and am not sure how to proceed. This usually happens when I want to stretch a group of already sophisticated writers in some way. (You know, the group of students who do and try everything we teach them, and we think, *Okay, what now?*) Here are three of Clark's strategies I find especially helpful:

- *Tool 5: Watch those adverbs.* Use them to change the meaning of the verb.
- *Tool 26: Use dialogue as a form of action.* Dialogue advances narrative; quotes delay it.
- *Tool 27: Reveal traits of character.* Show characteristics through scenes, details, and dialogue.

You will also find "string" for small-group conferences in these resources:

- The Craft Pause pages throughout *Study Driven* (2006), by Katie Wood Ray.
- The Writers Voices On . . . pages throughout *The Writing Workshop* (2001), by Katie Wood Ray with Lester Laminack.
- *Inside Writing: How to Teach the Details of Craft* (2005), by Donald Graves and Penny Kittle.
- *The Writer: The Essential Resource for Writers Since 1887.* (A magazine devoted to writing).
- Poynteronline (www.poynter.org). Although Poynteronline is designed specifically to support the journalism community, I find the resources available on the website to be invaluable for teachers of writing. You can read the entire site strictly as a visitor and find writing advice from the Poynter faculty as well as links to other websites. "Chip on Your Shoulder" is one of my favorite columns that I visit over and over again for tips such as, "The Best Writing Tip of All Time" and "What is Narrative Anyway?"

To sum up: I rip pages out of magazines. I dog-ear book pages and festoon them with sticky notes. I photocopy student work. I photocopy my own work. I save string. The string becomes the teaching tools I use to teach (or reteach) students in small-group conferences.

Establishing a
Predictable Structure

Mornings in the Slaughter household are always interesting. Tim and I manage to get ourselves dressed, fed, and ready for the day and get our two daughters—Emme, who is four, and Ella, who is six—off to their respective schools somewhat on time (getting to our schools on time is a different story). I know there are millions of families who accomplish this task every day without so much as a blip on the radar screen, but getting my family up and out and ready each morning can be one of the most difficult things I do.

Our most successful mornings are those in which we follow our morning routine. I lay out the girls' clothes, hair ties, socks, shoes, and hairbrush, while Tim prepares the breakfast and lunches. We wake the girls. They eat their breakfast. While I get them dressed and ready, Tim puts all the backpacks, work bags, laptops, and such into the cars. The girls brush their teeth and we are all off to the races. We follow our routine.

Unfortunately, I know this because there are days when we do not follow our routine. Tim must be at work extra early. The girls wake up "a little crusty," refusing to cooperate. One of us oversleeps (usually me). On these days, our mornings are utter chaos.

I believe in routines. Having a routine is crucial to my emotional well-being. I think having a way things go helps make the difficult less difficult and more manageable. The same holds true for our teaching. If we can establish routines, a way things go, we not only make our job manageable but also will very likely accomplish it successfully.

Structure is the key to making small-group work manageable. Backed by a way things go, we think, *I can do this.* Predictability and consistency bring about rhythm and automaticity so that the conference structure becomes second nature, just part of what we do. We are able to direct our energy and excitement toward more complex issues: What skill will we teach? How will we teach it? What will we need to be able to teach it?

Because I have found great success in following the conference structures outlined in Calkins' *The Art of Teaching Writing* (1994) and Calkins, Hartman, and White's *One to One* (2005), I leaned on those familiar structures when establishing the structure for the small group work presented here.

Get Students' Attention

Capturing students' attention is key. Because the children in a small-group conference outnumber the teacher, it is crucial to take a bit of time up front to establish simple, clear rules. For example, when I work with a small group of children in a writing conference, I want them to have a piece of their own writing in front of them, their pencil lying ready, eyes on me. I don't want them reading their piece or adding to it; I don't want them reading someone else's piece or writing their comments on it. Granted, I rarely say, "Here are the rules for our group. Rule 1. . . ." Instead, I say something like, "Writers, can you flip your piece over, place your pencil down, and look this way?" While I say those words, I model these actions with my own piece of writing and my own pencil. Here are some additional attention-getting prompts:

- Writers, may I have your attention?
- Writers, please look this way.
- Writers, pencils down and eyes on me for a moment.

I expect my students to internalize this behavior very quickly. After one or two conferences, they know they are expected to turn their piece over and place their pencil down the moment I begin to speak.

Compliment and Connect with Students

When I first began conducting small-group conferences in writing workshop, I omitted the compliment. How could I give an authentic compliment to a group? No, I'd need to compliment each student in the group individually, which would take too long.

But the truth is, kids are much more receptive to our teaching if we compliment them first. It's that simple. And there are other reasons I believe we should strive to compliment our students, even in small groups, the majority of the time.

Compliments bring enthusiasm to the group and raise the energy level. Compliments help us angle our thinking toward a strength-based approach, not a deficit-based one. Offering compliments helps us get better and better at explicitly naming the skill or strategy a student writer has applied. When we begin our conversation in small groups with a compliment, we model the way we hope our students will talk about writing with one another. Group compliments also strengthen relationships and the sense of belonging. Because most small groups in writing workshop are fluid and heterogeneous, students often get a chance to work with peers they may not have otherwise.

The compliment also helps children connect with the conversation at hand. They know we've called them together for a connected purpose. Authentic compliments contribute to student accountability for good work. The implicit message is, When you write, I read your writing and I notice things and I tell you about what I notice. I am noticing this in your work and yours and yours.

Here are some ways to give a compliment.

- Writers, I noticed you all were doing some smart work. [Describe something they were doing successfully.]
- I called you all together today because I was so thrilled that you were all [describe something they were doing successfully].
- When I was reading over your shoulders, I was so happy to see that you were [describe something they were doing successfully].

After giving the compliment, we can then connect it to a focus of the unit of study (This is important because . . .; This fits with what we know about . . .) and make a smooth transition to our teaching point (Because you are already doing this smart work, I think you are ready to . . .).

Introduce a Teaching Point

Of course, the purpose of a small-group conference is to teach the students something new or remind them of a writing skill, technique, or behavior that we have already taught. Either way, our teaching needs to be clear and specific.

So we start off by telling the kids what we're going to teach them.

- What I want to teach you, then, is. . . .
- I'm thinking you are ready to learn how to. . . .
- I want to give you a tip about. . . .
- I want to remind you that. . . .

Then we have to make good on our promise. When we say, "I want to teach you that we writers often reread our writing, paying special attention to verbs, because our verbs often help our reader picture characters and what is happening," it follows we will then teach (or reteach) this small group a strategy for doing that. We can demonstrate using our own writing (or that of a published author or a student), thinking aloud as we explain specifically what we mean.

The method of teaching we choose depends on the level of support the students need. If the students need a ton of support, a demonstration accompanied by a lot of thinking aloud is appropriate. If the students need only a nudge, we can show an example or remind them to use an existing resource (a chart hanging on the wall, for example). The more specific we are in our teaching, the more successful our students will be in their practice and application of the teaching point.

Regardless of the method of teaching I choose, I break up the skill or strategy into steps. Just as structure helps me manage my teaching, if I give my students structured support in the writing process, they too will think, *I can do this*. If I am demonstrating the teaching point about concentrating on verbs, I might say, "Watch me do this work. I'll reread my writing, paying special attention to the verbs. I'll circle the verbs in my sentence. I'll close my eyes and picture the action. I'll try to jot two or three other verbs that might better describe the action of my character and choose the one I think works best in my piece."

Then I apply the strategy to a story I am writing, thinking aloud as I model each step. "Okay, I'll read this sentence paying attention to the verb. Oh, here is the verb, it's the word that shows action. I'll circle it. Okay, now I'm going to close my eyes and picture the action. Hmmm. Let me think of another verb that might describe the action. . . ."

Ways to begin to teach/reteach include:

- Let me show you what I mean.
- Watch me as I do this work.
- Notice the way I. . . .
- Remember I taught you that. . . .
- Let's take a look at the steps on this chart.

I often wrap up my teaching by restating what I just taught: "Did you see what I just did? If I want my reader to picture the action (I always do!), I can reread my writing, paying special attention to the verbs by circling them, get a picture of the action in my mind, jot down two or three other verbs that might work, and circle the one that fits best in my story. So, let's all give this a try."

Coach Students as They Work

After we've stated our teaching point and demonstrated specifically what the skill or strategy entails, the focus of the conference shifts to the individual students in the group and the text in front of them. Our job now becomes coaching the students as each one applies the strategy in her or his work. All of the students should start working immediately, not wait for us to get them started one by one. I say something like, "Go ahead and get started. Don't wait for me." I motion for the children to pick up their pencils, and begin. Then I turn my attention to the child I will work with first, expecting the other children to write independently. Again, students will soon do this automatically. The more they participate in small-group conferences, the less you'll experience problems related to focus and productivity.

Prompts to encourage students to practice the teaching point include:

- Let's all practice this in our writing.
- Now I want you to try this.
- Think about the piece in front of you. How can you use what you've just learned to make it better?

- *Get students' attention*
  Writers, can I have your attention?
  Writers, can you look this way?
  Writers, pencils down and eyes on me for a moment.

- *Compliment students*
  Writers, I noticed you all were doing some smart work as you were. . . .
  When I was reading over your shoulders, I was so happy to see that you were. . . .

  - *and connect what they are doing to your purpose*
    This is important because. . . .
    This fits with what we know about. . . .

- *Introduce a teaching point*
  What I want to teach you, then, is. . . .
  I'm thinking you are ready to learn how to. . . .
  I want to give you a tip about. . . .
  I want to remind you that. . . .

  - *and then demonstrate how to apply it*
    Let me show you what I mean.
    Watch me as I do this.
    Notice the way I. . . .
    Remember I taught you that. . . .

- *Coach individual students*
  Make sure all the students are working on their pieces during this time, not waiting until you talk with them.

- *Link the work to the writing process*
  Writers, what I just taught you, you can use anytime you're writing and you. . . .
  I hope you always remember to. . . .
  Raul, I hope you remember what you are doing right now whenever you're. . . .

Figure 5.1   Small-Group Conference Structure in a Nutshell

Link the Work to the Writing Process

After coaching students as they work individually, we should again get everyone's attention and restate the teaching point, stressing its wider applicability:

- Writers, what I just taught you, you can use anytime you're writing and you. . . .
- I hope you always remember to. . . .

We can also do this as part of our individual coaching: "Raul, I hope you remember what you are doing right now whenever you're. . . ."

The teachers in my district and I spent a lot of time trying out various structures for small-group work. I share this structure not as the *only* effective structure but as the one we found the most successful with any type of group, made up of students of any age. As Roy Peter Clark (2006) stresses in his *Writing Tools: 50 Essential Strategies for Every Writer*, this structure is a tool, not a rule. Over time, it will become automatic. With time, you will discover your own variations.

The structure I use for small-group conferences is summarized in Figure 5.1. If you keep a copy in your conferring notebook, you'll have a prompt ready at hand until your conferences become second nature. It's also a good idea to practice small-group conferences with your colleagues. Imagine you're with a group of students. How would it go? Use the prompts to guide you.

Table Conferences

Most teachers arrange their classroom so that children are sitting at tables or at desks pushed together in clusters. In a setup like this, the groups for table conferences preexist naturally. We can join a table or cluster and confer with the students sitting there. In Calkins' *Units of Study for Teaching Writing, Grades 3–5* (2006) series, these are called "table conferences." This also means table groups will typically be heterogeneous.

For a table group conference, I step up to the group of students knowing that some (but perhaps not all) need help with the strategy. However, all of them will profit from participating in the conference. Typically, I find a small patch of table or desk on which to rest my things. Once I have the attention of the group, I'll teach, reinforce, or remind students of a strategy writers use. Then the students might have a conversation about the strategy and how it applies to their writing. Finally, I coach individual students at the table as they try out the strategy.

A Classroom Snapshot

It's Wednesday. Ms. Lucente, a first-year kindergarten teacher, has recently launched a how-to unit of study in her writing workshop. In her minilesson, Ms. Lucente demonstrates writing about how to make a peanut butter and jelly sandwich. As she demonstrates, she gestures thoughtfully, raising her eyes to the ceiling when deep in thought, putting up a finger as she calls out each step.

Then she gives each child several sheets of "how-to paper" and they are off to their tables. Ms. Lucente walks around the room, observing and admiring the children's work. She stops often, asking, "How's it going?" She approaches the red table. Circling it, she notes that all five children have drawn a picture in the box and started writing words on the first page. She kneels down, eye level. "Writers, can I ask you to stop what you are doing for a moment and put your eyes on me?" She waits while Dominic drops and retrieves his pencil. When she has everyone's attention, she says, "Writers, I noticed as I was reading your books that each one of you sat down and got right to work. You started drawing your picture in your first box and some of you have already added words. You know something big and important about writing on your own, don't you? Now I want to remind you about something we already know as writers—that it's helpful to plan how our books will go. One way we can do this is by touching each page and saying what we'll write there. Watch me do this with my how-to-make-a-peanut-butter-and-jelly-sandwich book."

Ms. Lucente pulls out her book. She demonstrates touching each page and planning how her book will go.

"Writers, this is a strategy we can use anytime we write. We can plan how our writing will go, not just on page one but on the next and the next. Let's all try this work today. Will each one of you think how your book will go by touching each page and saying out loud what you'll write? I'll come around the table and admire your planning work."

Isabella returns to drawing her picture, and Ms. Lucente gives a quick reminder: "Isabella, first we'll touch each page and plan. Then, we'll go back and write. Touch the first page and plan what you'll write." Isabella touches the first page and says, "How to line up for P.E."

"Very good, Isabella. You are making a plan for your book! Keep going."

Next Ms. Lucente crouches down next to Javier. Javier is touching each page with the tip of his pencil and talking out loud: "Put the piece of bread together."

"Javier? Are you writing a book about how to make a peanut butter and jelly sandwich like I am?" Javier nods. "And you are thinking about what you will write before you write it. Nice, Javier, you know that writers make a plan for their writing."

Ms. Lucente moves on to Dominic, who is touching his first page and saying, "One day I fed my dogs. Their names are Cashew and Peanut."

"Dominic. I know you have two dogs. You probably know how to do many things with your dogs. What are you planning to teach your reader how to do?"

"I don't know."

"You told me you feed your dogs, right? I don't have dogs. I'm wondering how you feed them?"

"I just get their bowls, one big one and one little one. I fill them with food. Dry food and that chicken stuff—you know that stuff?" He puts his hands together and pulls them apart to articulate the chicken stuff.

"Dominic, you know what I'm thinking? Since you know so much about how to feed your dogs, you could write your how-to book about feeding dogs. That's what writers do sometimes, we think, what do I know how to do that I could teach to other people? Do you want to try it?" Dominic nods. "When we're writing our how-to books, we often think, *What do I do first . . . and next . . . and next.* Can you touch each page and do that work?"

Dominic jumps right in. "First, I get the bowls, one big one and one little one." He turns to the next page. "Then . . ."

Ms. Lucente turns her attention to Nevea. . . .

When to Conduct Table Conferences

When Launching a New Unit of Study

Recently I was working in Mrs. Stevens' kindergarten class. The students had just wrapped up three units of study in a row on narrative writing and were now beginning a unit on all-about books. The first day, they browsed many examples of the genre while Mrs. Stevens pointed out the features of all-about books.

Then Mrs. Stevens presented a minilesson on how to choose a topic they knew a lot about, were experts in. She included examples of appropriate topics as well as inappropriate ones.

Still, it was no surprise that when the students began writing their own all-about books, more than half the class began by writing, "One day . . .," the phrase that immediately gets kids telling stories about moments that happened. Therefore, Mrs. Stevens and I began meeting with the children in table

Figure 6.1 Cameron's Tiger Piece

conferences to teach them a strategy for moving away from narrative or story language and beginning to use nonnarrative language. We taught the children to keep their topic foremost in their mind and begin each sentence with the topic they were writing about. For example, since Cameron was writing a book about tigers, she began, "Tigers have lots of stripes." (See Figure 6.1.)

Coaching students in small groups on those first days when they are writing in a new genre, will set them up to do good work for the rest of the unit. Imagine trying to do that work one student at a time?

When Reminding Students About Strategies We've Already Taught

Writing and reading teachers familiar with the architecture of the minilesson recognize its effectiveness as a vehicle for presenting clear and explicit instruction. I particularly love the moment in the minilesson when we link it to the bigger picture—when we remind students that our teaching is not just for today but for anytime: "So, I hope you'll always remember you can use this strategy whenever you sit down and write." We say it. We mean it. And often we forget it. And so do our students. We can do better. One way is to have a table conference reminding students of the work that has come before today and how it applies to any kind of writing.

I was reminded of the ups and downs of the learning curve just recently. My daughter Ella has been "reading" books for quite a while. *No Matter What* (Gliori 1999) is an "every night" book she has been reciting word for word from memory for years. Even when I'm out of town, I read the book aloud to Ella and Emme over the phone.

A month ago we sat down on the couch to read it yet again. Ella began saying the words of the story much more slowly and hesitantly than she usually does. Coming to the page on which the text reads, "'No matter what?' said Small with a smile. 'What if I were a crocodile?'" she struggled with nearly every word. When she came to the word *crocodile* she stopped, looked at me, and pointed to her ear, her signal that she wanted me to whisper the word to her. And I was thinking, "Hello? Earth to Ella. You know this book by heart!"

But Ella's kindergarten class had been learning to decode words by sounding them out. She was in the middle of the learning curve, focusing so much on sounding out each word that she completely forgot about the meaning of the book—a book she knew every word of by heart—and didn't so much as glance at the picture of the huge smiling crocodile! A few nights later, however, Ella was back to using all of her cueing systems.

Children are always somewhere within the learning curve. Part of our job as teachers is to teach them new strategies (for Ella, decoding words); another part is to remind them to use the strategies they already know (paying attention to meaning, rhyme patterns, picture clues). Table conferences are the perfect venue for reminding students of those strategies we want them to use again and again and again.

When Introducing a Layered
or Challenging Writing Technique

Many times when I'm preparing to teach a class a writing technique or skill I think, *This is a lot of thinking to hold on to.* I know it will be a stretch for many writers. But I teach it anyway, because I know it will be within the students' grasp at some point. Some understand and use the technique that very day. Others need more time. Whenever the point I'm teaching seems like a lot to hold on to, I hold table conferences. After the students return to their seats, I approach a table and provide a heavier scaffold, use a different teaching tool, and/or add a layer to the minilesson.

Recently I was working with a first-grade teacher who was presenting a poetry unit. In the whole-class minilesson I taught the students about Georgia Heard's "doors of poetry," specifically that writers open the door to their heart to find ideas for their poems. Because I wanted to keep my minilesson short and focused on ideas, I listed ideas for poems in my demonstration but I didn't take one of those ideas and then write a poem. However, following the minilesson, I met with groups of students at their tables and expanded the minilesson by teaching them a strategy for looking at a list of ideas and then writing a poem.

When Presenting a Variation on a Minilesson (You Could Also Try . . .)

Mrs. Roe's second graders were studying mentor authors so that they could use the same techniques in their own writing. For several days, they'd been studying Jane Yolen's *Owl Moon* (1987). The day I visited, they learned that writers often use their senses to describe a setting, not just on one page but on lots of pages, in order to help the reader envision it. In the previous unit, on poetry, they had learned about similes.

In her table conferences, Mrs. Roe taught her students that they could describe the setting using their senses, the way Jane Yolen does; that they could describe the setting using similes; and that they could combine these approaches. She carried her copy of *Owl Moon* with her, showed them how Jane Yolen did this, and coached them while they tried it themselves.

When Sharing a Student's Work

It was April in Mrs. Robinson's third-grade classroom. She launched a unit of study on the literary essay by teaching her students to "walk in the character's shoes" by envisioning a character and then writing about him or her in their notebook. She suggested that they begin their entries with the words *I can see.*

Researching the room, Mrs. Robinson noticed that Zachary was writing about the central character, Kevin, in Eloise Greenfield's *She Come Bringing Me That Little Baby Girl* (1974) as if he *were* Kevin. She shared Zachary's strategy with the other students at the table where Zachary was sitting and coached Zachary's tablemate Makayla as she tried the strategy in her own notebook.

When Sharing a One-to-One Conference From Which Everyone Will Benefit

Jennifer Pellerin's first graders were focusing on making sure readers could understand their stories. Jennifer approached Kayla for a one-to-one conference.

"Hi, Kayla. What are you working on as a writer today?"

Kayla showed Jennifer how she had checked the classroom word wall to find out how to spell a word correctly.

Jennifer applauded, then said, "Just a minute, Kayla. What you are telling me right now, I'm thinking everyone at your table needs to hear. Let me get their attention. Writers, can you put your pencils down for a moment and turn your eyes this way?" She waited while the other students at Kayla's table complied. "You know, Kayla is one of those writers who cares so much about her readers that she uses the word wall to make sure she has spelled her words correctly. Kayla, can you say more about that?"

Kayla explained that as she had reread her story, she thought the word *wut* didn't look right. Remembering that *what* was displayed on the word wall, she had checked it there, crossing out the misspelling and writing the correct spelling in the space above.

Jennifer said, "Isn't that smart, writers? Thumbs-up if you care about your readers the way Kayla does." The tablemates held up their thumbs. "Then you can use Kayla's strategy, too. Anytime you are writing or reading your writing, you can check the word wall to make sure your words are spelled correctly."

Tips for Conducting Table Conferences

I often recommend that teachers examine their students' writing and ask, "What is something we've been studying as writers about which my students

Qualities of Good Writing	Possible Table Conferences for _____Unit of Study
• Choosing topics/ideas • Sketching/labeling to plan, hold meaning, include details • Showing, not telling • Elaborating/adding details (internal thinking, dialogue, small action, physical setting, buddy sentences, descriptive sentences, facts, anecdotes, examples) • Revising (reread for meaning, choose the best word, add, take out, explode a moment) • Establishing voice • Maintaining focus: small moment, one idea, one event • Organizing/creating a structure: beginning, middle, end; table of contents; headings/subheadings • Using conventions: capitalization, end punctuation • Using correct spelling: high-frequency words, word walls • Writing with increasing volume/stamina/independence	

Figure 6.2   Planning Table Conferences

need more instruction?" Typical answers include tighter focus, better elaboration, use of conventions. These qualities of good writing are not genre specific. Preparing a chart like the one in Figure 6.2 will help you plan these kinds of conferences.

For example, recently I worked with a group of first-grade teachers preparing to teach a poetry unit. After studying some of the qualities of good writing they had been teaching earlier in the year, they identified the following table conference possibilities:

- using poetry paper with a sketch box and label, and adding details of the sketch to the poem
- using appropriate end punctuation (periods, question marks, exclamation points)
- writing longer poems

Another thing to remember is that you can practice your group conference skills by reinforcing the same quality at a number of tables. Keep your cheat sheet (Figure 5.1) with you if you need it.

Skill Conferences

As we saw in Chapter 6, table groups are heterogeneous and preexist; we don't form them based on a needs assessment. In contrast, all members of a skill group have the same specific strength or need. Having determined (through researching the room, reading students' ongoing writing, and making informal assessments) what these students need to know to grow as writers, we can use a skill conference to offer them guided practice in a very specific skill or writing technique, focusing on *how to implement* the strategy, so that these students will then be able to use the skill or technique as appropriate when they are writing independently.

Many teachers have a small round table at which groups gather for skill instruction (in reading, writing, math, whatever). Other teachers hold their skill conferences in a portion of the meeting area.

A Classroom Snapshot

The following conference took place in the middle of a unit of study on revising personal narratives. The day before, the teacher had collected a revised draft from each student and, using a rubric, assessed targeted writing skills and techniques. One of the specific writing skills she assessed was whether the students were focusing their stories around one idea or event.

On a Thursday morning in December, Rachel Tracy's first graders are writing. They sit at their tables, pencils in hand, working intently. Rachel is seated at one of the student tables writing her own story. After a few moments she gets up, walks through the room, and, stopping at various tables, asks Sophia, Reece, and Jalia to meet her on the rug for a conference. When the children gather, they place their stories behind them and sit with their eyes on Rachel.

"I read your stories last night," Rachel begins, "and I'm noticing you are really stretching yourselves as writers—writing more and more on each page and writing longer stories. We writers do that. We push ourselves to write even better and longer stories. We continue to stretch and outgrow ourselves as writers day after day. Good work.

"As we're stretching and growing as writers, it's important to remember all the important strategies we've learned in the past to keep our writing focused. Today, I want to remind you of something we writers often do whenever we're writing stories. We ask, 'What's this story about?' and then reread our story to make sure it shows this big thing. Watch me do this work."

Rachel picks up the story she's been working on and revisiting in whole-class minilessons as well as in conferences. Her students know the story well—it's about the time her son sprained his ankle. "First, I'll ask myself, 'What's the big thing my story is about?' That's easy. It's about the time Brendan sprained his ankle. Next, I'll touch each page, making sure each page of my story is about that big thing. Okay, first page." She touches the first page. "Is this page about Brendan spraining his ankle?" Page by page Rachel explicitly demonstrates the work she wants students in this group to try, making sure each page tells more and more about the big thing the story is about.

She then asks, "Will you try this work right now?" Her students pick up their pieces and practice the strategy they have just been shown. As they work, Rachel talks with each of them individually.

"How's it going, Reece?"

"I am writing a story about decorating the tree. The big thing is putting on the lights."

"How exciting!"

Reece then rereads his story and realizes he has written about decorating the tree on his first page, brushing his teeth on his second page, and going to bed on the third page. He decides to pull his story apart and add more pages about lighting the holiday tree. On his last page, he writes: "The lights twinkled on and off. It was beautiful!"

Jalia is already pulling the pages of her story apart and grabbing new pages from the pile Rachel has brought with her when Rachel approaches her. "I see you pulled your story apart and have some new pages. What are your plans?"

Jalia explains she is writing a story about the water balloon toss at the fall festival and has discovered that parts of it aren't about that big thing. "I'm just taking it apart and adding new pages here and here." She points to the new first and last page of her story.

"What are you going to write on your new pages?" Rachel asks.

"On this page I'm going to write about standing in line watching everyone get wet. And on this page I'm going to write about drying off with my mom's new jacket!"

After working briefly with Sophia as well, Rachel wraps up the conference by getting the three students' attention once more. "Writers, today I reminded you of something that we writers do even as we continue to stretch ourselves by writing longer and longer stories—we ask, 'What's this story about?' and reread it to make sure it's about that big thing."

When to Conduct Skill Conferences

Skill conferences are always useful. Our students can never get enough support when they are learning the strategies they need as writers, building on what they already know how to do, and improving their writing skills. But there are a number of situations in which skill conferences are especially effective.

When Addressing Patterns of Student Response

Chapter 3 describes ways teachers, in grade-level teams, can anticipate possible student responses. When I was working with the teachers at Bear Creek Elementary School, Mrs. Peacock was preparing to launch a unit on all-about books with her third graders. She decided to begin by having her students read a number of all-about books, notice common features, and note those features in their writer's notebooks. We anticipated that a number of children would write down facts rather than features.

Researching the room, we found five students who were recording facts from the books they were reading. I pulled these students together in a circle on the rug and reread my own notebook entries, asking myself, "Is this a feature of an all-about text, something I'd probably find in tons of other all-about books, or is this a fact, something that teaches me about the topic that I'd only find in a book on this topic?" Then I asked the students to ask themselves that same question about the things on their own list.

When Studying Craft

Barrie Evans' fourth graders were studying how writers grab the reader's attention with a strong lead. In one minilesson, Barrie taught her student how to write a picture-perfect lead (one that describes the setting). When the students went off to write, Barrie read over their shoulders, then taught a group of students how to add a simile to their picture-perfect lead, like Jane Yolen does in *Owl Moon*.

When Students Are Revising Their Work

Mrs. Pagliaro's fourth graders were writing essays. After teaching the elaboration strategy of telling a "ministory," she noticed that several students included a ministory that just listed actions. She taught this small group of students how to revise their ministory to include things like internal thinking and dialogue that help the reader envision the scene.

When Teaching Conventions

The best time to explain conventions is when students realize that things like punctuation are useful in helping readers understand their writing and are trying to use these conventions appropriately. However, they're usually all over the map in terms of specifics.

For example, everyone will probably need lessons on elaboration. And the whole class will profit from rereading their piece and asking, "Does this make sense?" But we needn't teach a whole class of fourth graders to capitalize the first letter in a sentence; most of them are well aware of this convention. The handful of students who aren't can receive guided practice and coaching in a small group. The same is true for advanced skills. It probably doesn't make sense to teach a whole class of first graders that writers use quotation marks to show the reader that a character is talking. But if we notice a handful of our first graders attempting to use quotation marks in their piece, we can help them learn how to do it correctly as a small group.

When Working with Students in the Same Stage of the Writing Process

Mrs. Casey's second graders were in the middle of a unit on revising narratives. On the day I visited her class, she taught her students ways to revise when there isn't any room to revise: writing a sentence on a strip of paper and taping the strip to the story, or adding a whole new page. When the students went off to work on their own, most of them began adding to a story already in progress. However, three students started a new story that day (something the class always has the option of doing).

Mrs. Casey and I gathered the three students who were in the planning stage of the writing process and taught (really, *reminded*) them that writers touch each page and plan how the story will go and that a good way to do this is to touch the middle page and think about the big feeling or main action, then touch the first page and think about what happened just before, and finally touch the last page and think about what happened after. I demonstrated by planning a story about seeing a cockroach on the kitchen floor and then asked them to follow the same process in planning their own story.

When Students Are Reflecting on Their Current Writing and Setting Goals for Future Writing

We can form a group of students who have common goals for their writing and teach them strategies for meeting those goals.

Tips for Conducting Skill Conferences

Chapter 3 discusses several methods of assessing children for the purpose of forming small groups. Some teachers find choosing among several assessment methods overwhelming: Where do I start? The simplest method for forming small groups for skill conferences is in relation to the teaching point of the day's minilesson.

On a clipboard paper, make three columns:

Who in this class is doing this now?

Who in this class is almost doing this now?

Who in the class is *not* doing this now?

- One strategy I use when I want to write a story filled with emotion or tension is to remember a time in my life filled with worry or trouble. Let me show you what I mean . . .
- One thing I want to teach you is that writers often ask, "What do I really want to say?" Once we've decided what the story is really about we ask, "How can I show this to my readers?"
- Writers often craft several leads that "hook" the reader and choose the one that works best for their story.
- Writers help their readers visualize by adding details about the physical description of the characters.
- Writers reveal traits of characters by using description: what the character does or says and through use of physical description. Instead of writing, "She was brave," we might write: "She stood in front of the audience. 'I won't back down now,' she whispered."
- Writers can ask themselves, "How is the character feeling?" and "What might they say to show that feeling?"
- Writers help their readers visualize by adding details about the setting.
- Writers often revise by sketching the character in the setting and ask, "Why did I draw it that way?" The answers to that question often lead to revision work.
- Writers, something I do when I'm revising is I reread my work looking for words that repeat (for example, beginning each sentence with the word *I*) and I ask myself, "Did I do this on purpose?" If the answer is no, as it often is, I revise my work in order to vary my sentences/words. Watch me do this . . .
- Writers search for "too general" words (*good/nice/fun*) and revise to be more specific.
- Writers, sometimes I flip through my last few (drafts/notebook pages) searching for patterns. I ask myself, "Do I always do things this way?" And then I try to push myself to do something differently. Look, I noticed I always begin my story with the words "One day . . ."
- One thing we can do to bring our voice (or the voices of our characters) to our writing is to practice saying our dialogue out loud and use punctuation to help our reader understand not just *what* was said, but *how* it was said.
- Writers can make our writing more lively and interesting by varying the length of our sentences. Instead of short-short-short or long-long-long, we try short-long-short.

Figure 7.1   Potential Skill Conference Topics for a Variety of Ages

Research the room for about five minutes, jotting down names in the appropriate columns. A sure bet for a skill conference is to gather the students who are *almost* doing the work. After you have their attention, a natural compliment is to commend them for giving the strategy a try. Then begin your conference: "Now that you've given it a try, let's practice a way to make it even better. . . ." Figure 7.1 will give you some additional ideas for skill conferences.

Once you're comfortable forming groups in relation to the day's teaching point, you'll be ready and eager to try the other methods.

Expectation Conferences

W e've all been in classrooms in which the tables and folders are color-coded, pencils are freshly sharpened in a jar, the kids' backpacks hang from hooks, the books in the classroom library are neatly stacked in labeled bins, there's not a loose paper in sight, and the students are engaged and working productively. And we know that when we walk into this same teacher's classroom next year and the year after that, the students will be different but the sense of order and efficiency will be the same.

These teachers are not privy to some ancient wisdom, nor do they have magical tricks up their sleeve; they have expectations for the way things will go, and more important, they teach their students how to manage materials and monitor themselves. This does not happen overnight. But it does happen.

Group conferences are an effective and efficient way to teach students how to meet classroom expectations. Expectation conferences can be held with either skill (homogeneous) groups (see Chapter 7) or table (heterogeneous) groups (Chapter 6).

A Classroom Snapshot

Mrs. Wiseman's fourth-grade classroom is filled with the satisfying sounds of children writing. Pencils scratch. Pages turn. Children fill up their pages with the stories of their lives. Except for Billy. And Sheeka. And Christopher. Billy is drawing a continuous spiral around and around and around in his notebook. Sheeka and Christopher stare at the blank pages in front of them.

Mrs. Wiseman, a first-year teacher, gives me a worried look and whispers, "I don't know what to do. This happens almost every day."

Mrs. Wiseman is wise to worry. This is a situation teachers—first year, third year, thirty-third year—face all the time. My response is as honest and simple as it is complex and sticky. "It is an expectation that students write every day during writing workshop. That's the simple part. But there is the matter of coming up with an idea. And some kids do struggle with this. But mostly, kids *could be* brimming with ideas but put forth so much energy avoiding writing they never even try. This is learned behavior. I have a colleague who says that at the heart of avoidance lies fear. Therefore, everything we do, especially early in the year, should send this message, loudly and clearly: *Nothing bad will ever happen to you in this classroom. In fact, when you write, we will celebrate, and good things will happen.* That's the more layered and complex part."

After our conversation, Mrs. Wiseman meets with Billy, Sheeka, and Christopher in a small group. "Writers, I called you all over to the rug today because I noticed the three of you doing some smart work. All of you were deep in thought. Writers do that. We think. Thinking is important, isn't it? But sometimes I think and think and think so hard that I can't think of anything. Writers often call this writer's block. Does that ever happen to you?" The students nod yes. "What I want to tell you today is so important that I hope you remember it always: the very act of writing—writing anything—helps writers with writer's block come up with ideas. We have to stop thinking and just write. Writers, this is why it is an expectation during our writing workshop that you write. It's not okay for you to sit and just think and think and think. To avoid writer's block, you must write and write and write. I'm going to teach you three strategies I use whenever I am faced with writer's block. That way, if you ever have writer's block again, you can use one of these strategies.

"Here they are. I can write about what happened the moment I rolled out of bed this morning. I can write about what happened right before I went to bed last night. I can write about something that happened to me on my way to school this morning. Let me pick one. I'll write about something that happened the moment I rolled out of bed this morning. Okay, let me think. . . ." Mrs. Wiseman demonstrates coming up with a story idea and jotting it down in her notebook.

Then she says, "Writers, now I want each one of you to practice this strategy. Even if you've already thought of a story idea to write about, I want you to pretend you still have writer's block and your mind is empty. Instead of sitting there and thinking and thinking and thinking, making your writer's block worse and worse and worse, choose a strategy. You can choose to write about something that happened right when you rolled out of bed, right before you went to bed, or something that happened on the way to school today. Make your choice and begin writing."

Next, Mrs. Wiseman works with each student individually, showering them with compliments.

"Christopher, what did you choose?"

"I am writing about what happened on the bus this morning. I almost missed it."

"Oh, no! Then what happened?"

When all the children are writing, Mrs. Wiseman says, "Writers, can I have your attention for just one more second? Before you go back to your seats and continue writing, I want to remind you of what you just learned. You've learned that it is an expectation that during writing workshop we all write. Even if you have writer's block, you will still write. You've learned that the way to face writer's block is not to sit and sit and sit and think and think and think. No, the way to face writer's block is to write and write and write even more. Anytime you have writer's block, you can use this strategy. Get yourself writing by writing about something that happened right when you rolled out of bed this morning, something that happened right before you went to bed last night, or something that happened on the way to school today. I'm going to jot those ideas down on a chart and hang them right here in the room should you ever need to refer to them again."

When to Conduct Expectation Conferences

When Establishing Expectations in the Beginning of the Year

Our best cues for how to establish expectations come from kindergarten teachers. They tell their students what to do, show them how to do it, and tell them what they just did, *all day long*. They do it when they want kids to line up at the door. They do it when they want kids to put their backpacks away. They do it when they want kids to get out their pencil and paper. They make charts with pictures, establish color codes, sing songs—they pull out all of the stops. And they don't give up until the children follow the expectations appropriately. I am in awe of kindergarten teachers.

During the second week of school, Ms. Lance's kindergarten students were writing. Crayons in hand, they were remembering moments of their lives and sketching those moments on the page. After a few minutes, an "I'm done!" erupted out of Cameron. Right after that Mikayla jumped out of her seat, story in hand, "I'm done, too!" Ms. Lance approached the table and knelt down. "Writers, may I have your attention?" Ms. Lance complimented the students on their stories. Then she reminded her young writers that when writers finish one story they have choices. She pointed to the chart she had created in her whole-class minilesson: What We Do When We Think We're Done. The chart listed choices with pictures illustrating those choices: Add to the story or start a new story. Ms. Lance then pretended she was done with her piece of writing. "Okay. I'm done!" she said as if to herself. "Hmm. What should I do? I know! I can announce it to the class. But wait a minute, that might disrupt the other writers. Hmm. I know. I have choices. It says so right there on the chart. I can add to my story or start a new one. I think I'll start a new one. On the chart it shows a basket in the middle of the table with paper. Here it is right here in the middle of my table!"

We teach the whole-class minilessons about our expectations for classroom routines. And then we observe. The majority of our students will profit when we teach and reteach and reteach our expectations in small groups until our workshop looks, sounds, feels, and is productive.

When Helping Students Who Have Difficulty Following Expectations

Mrs. Cotilla's second graders were expected to work with a writing partner at different times during the workshop. They sat with their special writing partner during the minilesson, they met with their writing partner frequently during independent writing, and they sat with their writing partner during the share session.

Two of the writing partnerships rarely talked with each other. Before reassigning partners, Mrs. Cotilla gave these four students explicit instruction about how to talk to one another about writing. In a small-group conference, she taught them that writing partners start with a friendly greeting ("Hello. How's it going with your writing today?"), take turns reading part or all of the piece, compliment each other, and offer a suggestion. Then she coached the partnerships as they worked through these steps. They were then able to work in a much more productive way.

When Helping Students Who Rely on You to Get Them Started

In writing workshop students spend most of the time writing independently. And there are always a few students who wait for us to get them started. I visited Mrs. Bowen's fifth-grade classroom on a Friday afternoon. Her students were learning about building a portfolio of work. After the minilesson, we sent the students off to read through their current work and choose which pieces they wanted to include in their portfolio. Five students had their hands up before they even sat down. Mrs. Bowen whispered to me that their behavior was typical.

I gathered the five students on a corner of the rug and reminded them about the three *S* expectations: that during the workshop all writers would be *seated*, *silent*, and *self-reliant*.

"If every once in a while you find yourself walking back to your desk confused, no big deal. This happens to writers, readers, mathematicians, scientists. We're not sure. We're confused. Sometimes the very act of doing something gets our brains warmed up and cranking. Eureka! We figure it out. However, if you find yourself confused and not sure what to do a lot of the time, this may indicate that you are not paying attention when Mrs. Bowen is teaching you skills and strategies."

Then I shared a few strategies writers use to be self-reliant even when they aren't sure what to do.

1. Read the charts around the room for clues.
2. Peek at your tablemates. What are they doing?
3. If all else fails, start a new entry in your notebook.

I asked the students to try out those steps then and there. Most of them were able to begin working independently simply by rereading the chart posted in the room!

When Introducing a New Classroom Procedure

One January, Ms. Chin noticed that a few of her third-grade partnerships were working together especially well, listening to each other intently, giving each other specific compliments and constructive advice. She decided to offer these students a special privilege: They could grab their writing partner and meet in a special spot in the room at their discretion, without waiting until they were specifically asked to do so.

To introduce this new privilege, Ms. Chin called these students together and introduced a few simple procedures.

1. Check to see whether the special spot is available (there is only enough room for one partnership at a time).
2. Quietly give your partner the signal.
3. If your partner nods yes, meet in the spot.
4. Set the timer for no more than five minutes.

Then she asked the students to pretend they wanted to meet with their partner and simulate going through the steps.

When Helping Students Meet Deadlines

Many of the teachers I work with set a publication/celebration date at the beginning of a writing unit of study. Mrs. Dragon launched her fourth-grade poetry unit by saying, "Poets, for the next five weeks, we'll read and write tons of poems. At the end of this unit, we will celebrate by inviting your parents in to our classroom to listen to your beautiful poems read aloud and also for tea and cookies. Isn't this exciting?" As Mrs. Dragon made this announcement, she placed a special "Writing Celebration" tag on the classroom calendar.

For most children, this kind of goal provides the necessary impetus. Yet, despite all our preparation, teaching, and best intentions, four or five children will probably lag behind, missing deadlines, and, at the end of the unit, have nothing to publish. We can help students like this by teaching them goal-setting strategies.

The gist of such a small-group conference is this: "It is an *expectation* that by such and such date you will have such and such done. And I'm going to help you meet that expectation. Here's how. . . ." Then we teach the students to set goals for themselves. The particular goals depend on age or grade level. We can help our students set reasonable goals for pages, lines, number of words written per day. Or, especially in the upper grades, we can set goals related to the writing process. For example: By Friday, have drafts of at least ten poems in your notebook. Another good idea is to give each student a personal calendar they can keep in their writing folder and/or writer's notebook and ask them to set and jot down interim goals.

In no way am I saying we can expect all our students to be in the same place in their writing at the same time. We can't. And we certainly don't want to be regimented about the number of days students spend on each stage of a writing process that isn't linear. We never want to say, "Spend two days collecting ideas, one day developing, three days drafting, four days revising," and so forth. Writers often shift back and forth between stages, going back at points before moving forward.

As writing teachers, we *expect* our students to be in different places in the process. But we also expect our students to meet deadlines, and we can teach them strategies that will help them do so.

Revisiting Conference Structure

A Direct Approach

Recently I was working in a third-grade classroom. As I researched the room along with the teacher, I noticed a few students moving around during independent writing, interrupting others, and doing anything they could to avoid writing. I tried sending some nonverbal cues, like motioning for them to sit down and picking up an imaginary pencil and writing on an imaginary paper, but the behavior continued.

So I called the three students together for an expectation conference. It hardly seemed appropriate to begin with a compliment. I could have made one up, but the whole point of the compliment in a conference is to highlight something the children are doing well, something we hope they will continue to do in writing workshop. I did not want the children to continue doing any of the things they were doing. So instead of complimenting them, I decided to take a direct approach.

First, I made a *connection*. "Writers, we've been studying that writers often revise their work. Then I presented my *teaching point*. In order to do this work, writers need to be productive. I want to remind you what productive writing looks like. Writers are most productive when we are sitting in our chairs on our bottoms, our backs straight, our eyes focused on our work, writing."

"Watch me. I'll show you exactly what productive work looks like. Notice how I'm sitting straight and my eyes are focused on my writing?"

Next I began the *active engagement/coaching* part of the lesson. "Let's practice this work right here. Will you all show me and the rest of the group members what it looks like to be productive?"

Finally, I *linked* the teaching point to writing in general. "If we are to accomplish anything as writers—our entries, our drafts, our revisions—we must be productive. Today, you have learned what it looks like to be productive in our workshop. I want you to remember this and practice this every day when you write."

An Inquiry Approach

When I research the room during any given workshop, I often see one table of students who would benefit from a refresher conversation about classroom expectations. In these instances, I'll often begin my conference by having each student at that table answer the same question.

For example, suppose a table of students has done very little writing. I might begin something like this: "I was walking around the room paying close attention to the volume of writing in today's workshop. I'm noticing that the students at this table have each produced no more than three or four lines of writing. What's going on?"

After listening to their responses, I'll try to summarize. "So, what I hear most of you saying is that you were distracted by the constant squeaking of the wet shoe hitting the ground and it sort of pulled the whole group off track and you couldn't get your focus back."

I can then offer some direct advice: "Well, let me give you a few tips so that this doesn't happen again." Or I can allow the group members to solve the problem: "What are you going to do so that doesn't happen again?" With either method, I have the students practice the remedial actions. Then I conclude the conference by linking these actions to the writing process in general.

Tips for Conducting Expectation Conferences

First, of course, we need to observe our students as they work. But that's not the tricky part. Most teachers can tell you, precisely, who is doing what during writing workshop: "Steven, Makayla, and Desi get up, can't find their writer's notebook, search for things, sharpen their pencil—anything to avoid writing."

But once we know who's doing what, it helps to answer three questions.

1. *What do I want those students doing instead of what they are doing now?* I want the students to stay seated and writing.
2. *Why is this important?* To get better at anything (a skill, a hobby, a craft), we have to do that thing nearly every day for long stretches of time. Doing it regularly, we find a rhythm and we improve.
3. *How should they go about doing it?* Two or three minutes before writing workshop, I'll give these students a signal that tells them they should place two sharpened pencils and their notebook/folder on their desk and go to the bathroom if they need to.

Once we've answered the three questions, the point and structure of the expectation conference are both very clear. Also, remember that an expectation conference often requires that the students simulate behavior: "Writers, let's pretend it's time to work with your partner. Show me how partnership work goes in this classroom."

Progress Conferences

By now we are becoming experts on the topic of small-group work within the writing workshop. We realize the importance, value, and benefits of meeting with small groups of children, and we know there are an infinite number of reasons for doing so. We've learned about the different kinds of small groups and the purposes for meeting with those groups. We know that for the most part, these groups are fluid and homogenous and that they allow us to differentiate our instruction to meet varying student needs.

So far, I've suggested that we meet with this small group and that small group today and with another group and another tomorrow and still different ones next week. However, there are lots of times when we need to meet with the same group again and again, to check back and see how the students are doing. Meeting with Dylan, Kay Kay, Jacea, and R.J. on Wednesday, we say, "When we met on Monday, you were checking your end punctuation and making sure the very next letter following your end punctuation was a capital letter. How's that going for you? Are you trying that work out in the pieces you are working on today? Let's take a look." Progress conferences promote accountability. They also help students generalize strategies, use them every time they write.

A Classroom Snapshot

In the snapshot in Chapter 7, Rachel Tracy taught first graders Reece, Jalia, and Sophia that writers often ask themselves, "What's the big thing my story is about?" This progress conference with these same students took place a week later.

"A few days ago, we met together to talk about the stories you were writing. You all reread your stories and revised them, making sure your story was all about one big thing. Remember how Reece decided to revise his holiday tree story by adding new pages about hanging lights on it, instead of adding the part about what he did the next day?" The students nod. "What I want to tell you today is that we want to do this always and forever when we write. Even when we start brand-new stories, we want to ask ourselves that question: Is my story about one big thing? Watch. Let me show you."

Rachel starts a new story of her own, demonstrating how she makes sure it is all about one big thing by asking herself as she writes if the details she is adding are all about that same big topic.

Then she says, "Did you see what I did? I remembered a strategy that worked for me before, a really important strategy, and it worked for me again! Shall we all try this work? What do you think?" She holds up a thumb and nods her head; Reece, Jalia, and Sophia enthusiastically follow suit.

As Reece, Jalia, and Sophia work independently, Rachel moves among them, coaching and encouraging. Finally she says, "Let's do a quick share. Will each of you, in turn, tell the group the big thing your story is about and how you'll show that on each page?"

After the students take turns sharing, Rachel says, "Writers, always remember, this is an important strategy, asking yourself if your story is about just one big thing, and you can use it anytime you write—not just with the story you worked on last week, not just with today's story, but with any story. Okay?"

When to Conduct Progress Conferences

When Helping Students Meet Bottom-Line Standards
The bottom lines we want our writing curriculum to achieve (see Chapter 2) become specific goals for progress conferences with students who are not meeting them satisfactorily. Recently, I was working in a second-grade classroom where one bottom-line standard was to be able to write a focused narrative. Researching the room, the classroom teacher and I identified three

students who were writing "breakfast to bed" stories—essentially a long list of all the events of the day, from waking up in the morning (breakfast) until going to sleep at night (bed).

We knew a one-time small-group conference wouldn't miraculously lead these kids to be able to write focused narratives. Instead, we planned several conferences with them in which we would reteach the difference between a "watermelon topic" (the whole day) and a "seed idea" (one incident); remind them that writers often begin by planning the middle of the story first (What's the big thing that happened?), then frame it with what happened just before and just after that; and help them apply these concepts and strategies.

We didn't hold these conferences three or four days in a row. Instead, we met with the group every four or five days, allowing them plenty of time to practice and apply not only the skills they were learning as a group but also those they were learning in the whole-class minilessons.

When Helping Kids Keep Pace with the Class as a Whole

Almost every classroom includes a group of students who lag behind. They're easy to identify. They drag their feet in the morning. They roll their eyes. They doodle in their notebooks. They take too long getting started. When their classmates have written several sentences of a notebook entry, they're still writing down the date.

Kids are a lot like adults: some require more frequent accountability checks than others. Progress conferences, perhaps once a week, support kids who are working toward independence but aren't quite there yet. These conferences send two important messages. First: These things I'm teaching you every day, I expect you to go off and try. Then: I'm going to be talking with you about your work and asking for you to show me evidence of this work. Kids need to be accountable for their work and given the strategies to set and monitor their goals.

There are tons of strategies we can teach kids to increase their writing stamina. Obviously, they need to be able to choose their own topics, write about things they care about. They need to have a sense of purpose. They need to know who their audience is. We can cheer them on, especially early in the year, and celebrate the work they've done as writers. We can ask them to set goals for themselves—entries/pages/lines/stories written in a day, a week, a unit. Gradually, as we notice that the children are using the strategies and skills we've been teaching them, we can meet with the group less often.

Here's an example.

"I've called you together to review what it is we've been working on during the last few days in writing workshop. We're studying how to write feature articles. Remember, I taught you how to choose a topic and how to develop your topic by focusing on unusual or interesting ideas related to your topic. Finally, I taught you how writers often think about how their article might proceed from beginning to end: they consider a number of possibilities. We can list these steps as goals:

___ I chose a topic.
___ I fleshed out ideas.
___ I tried out different plans for how my article might go.

"Today, I'd like each of you to write these goals in your notebook. Once you've completed each step, place a check mark next to that step. Remember to use the strategy charts on the wall. Make it your personal goal to have this work completed today. Place your notebook on my table at the end of workshop so that I can admire your work! Get going!"

When Promoting Accountability: "I Care, I Remember, and My Words Matter"

One recent October, I was spending my first day in Mrs. Dunn's first-grade classroom. During independent writing, five hands shot up. Three of these children wanted help spelling a word. Calling them together as a group, I taught them that we writers are brave spellers, that instead of asking for help, we spell words all by ourselves. One way we can do this is by saying the word s-l-o-w-l-y (stretching it out), listening to the sounds we hear, and writing those sounds on our paper.

I returned to Mrs. Dunn's class a week later. During independent writing, Sharrod and Julianna, students in that original spelling group, again asked me for help spelling a word. Failures to remember like this happen all the time, and when they do, a progress conference is invaluable. I called Sharrod and Julianna to a corner of the rug. "Last week I met with you and taught you a strategy for being a brave speller. And you did such a good job practicing

Monday	Tuesday	Wednesday	Thursday	Friday
Goal	Goal	Goal	Goal	Goal
_____ I did it!	_____ I did it!	_____ I did it!	_____ I did it!	_____ I did it!

Figure 9.1   Goal Setting Calendar

that work. Remember? Sharrod, you stretched out the word *Walmart,* and Julianna, you stretched out the word *playground*. That was so brave and independent of you. We writers are like that, aren't we? So I was a little confused today when you each asked me to help you spell another word! That's why I want to remind you that the strategies I teach you are for anytime you write, not just for that day's work. From this day forward, forever and ever, you can be brave spellers! Let's practice that work again now."

Tips for Conducting Progress Conferences

During your Monday meeting with a group, give the members a weekly calendar (see Figure 9.1) and help them set goals for the week as writers: stories or entries written, lines written, movement through the writing process, time spent writing, whatever it is that will help these particular writers progress productively. Tell them you will meet with them on Wednesday to admire their progress and again on Friday to celebrate meeting the goals of the week.

The following week, try stretching the days between conferences, meeting Monday and again on Friday.

When we remember particular students' needs and keep checking on their progress, they realize that we care about the things we teach—and that we expect them to remember the things we've taught them.

Systematic Planning and Record Keeping

Planning

During "walk-throughs," our district supervisors, in order to evaluate the education our students receive, walk through classrooms with the school principal and administrative staff. The supervisors report their findings to the principal; the principal reports the findings to the teachers. The principal and teachers know the date of the walk-through far in advance, and they know to some degree what the supervisors are looking for: the district initiatives. (Principals often conduct mock walk-throughs to prepare for the official one.)

Some years ago one of the initiatives of our district was "The Flow of the Day": all the elementary teachers were supposed to post their daily schedule of instruction on the classroom wall where everyone could see it. I thought this was sort of silly, but it didn't conflict with any of my hard-and-fast beliefs about teaching and learning. Our school administrators even provided laminated subject tags. All I had to do was hang the tags up in the room in the right order and designate the time periods for each one. Mine looked something like this:

Morning Math Calendar	8:45–9:00
P.E.	9:00–9:30
Writing Workshop	9:40–10:40
Reading Workshop	10:40–11:40
Vocab/Word Work	11:40–12:10
Read-Aloud	12:10–12:35

Lunch	12:35–1:05
Math Workshop	1:10–2:10
Science/Social Studies	2:10–2:40

No big deal, right? But right there, for all to see, I was revealing one of my little secrets: I didn't love *everything* about teaching. Mostly, I loved teaching writing and reading. Math? Science? Social studies? Not so much. I also loved the "teachable moment." My reading and writing blocks could extend all day, and often did.

But once we were required to post our schedules and time allotments, I started teaching a full day of curriculum—not just the subjects I loved—pretty consistently. The district had been on to something. When we carve out specified times, our plans are a lot more likely to happen.

So our plan for small-group instruction should have times attached. Most teachers' writing blocks (for a more detailed discussion of the writing block, see Chapter 1) are between forty-five and sixty minutes long:

Explicit teaching (minilesson)	10–15 mintues
Writing and conferring	30–40 minutes
Sharing	5–10 minutes

The examples in this chapter assume thirty minutes spent writing and conferring. We can adjust this number up or down depending on our students, our grade level, the time of year, and the length of our writing block.

To begin, we can try having one one-to-one conference and one small-group conference each day of the week (Monday through Friday):

Research the room	5 minutes
One-to-one conference	5 minutes
Small-group conference	10 minutes

We'll decide with whom to have one-to-one conferences and what kind of small-group conferences to have based on the needs of our students. The more we become familiar with small-group conferring and the more we widen our assessment stance, the easier it becomes to determine who, when, and how we'll meet with our students.

However, we have to start somewhere. One way is to list five students who are struggling the most with writing right now and plan to meet with these students in our one-to-one conferences. We'll then also plan to have a conference with each of our table groups (or student teams). The plan would look like this:

Monday	Tuesday	Wednesday	Thursday	Friday
1–1: Giovani	1–1: Armani	1–1: Miranda	1–1: Natalia	1–1: Noah
Small-group conference: Table 1	Small-group conference: Table 2	Small-group conference: Table 3	Small-group conference: Table 4	Small-group conference: Table 5

Following the plan above, we will meet with all our students at least once during the week, and our five most struggling students twice. We just need to make sure we have no more than one conference with a student during a workshop. For example, if Giovani sits at Table 1, we won't have a one-to-one conference with Giovani *and* a conference with his table on the same day.

The following week, we can alternate table conferences and skill conferences.

Monday	Tuesday	Wednesday	Thursday	Friday
1–1: Giovani	1–1: Armani	1–1: Miranda	1–1: Natalia	1–1: Noah
Table conference: Table 1	Skill conference: Julian, Analisa, Javier, Ramone	Table conference: Table 3	Skill conference: Noah, Christopher, Ella, Payne	Table conference: Table 5

A bit of an aside here. A timer is an essential piece of classroom equipment. I've always timed classroom transitions, encouraging students to beat the time it took the day before. I've timed fluency checks, multiplication tests, classroom cleanups—you name it, I've timed it. However, I rarely timed *myself* doing anything in the classroom. I do now, and I highly recommend it. I start the timer when I begin a conference, and I push stop at the end. I don't set the timer to sound at a certain time, because I don't want to disrupt the work at hand. But I do want to know how long my conferences are so I can make sure kids are getting the benefit of my time.

Initially, small-group conferences might run fifteen or so minutes. With practice, however, that time will decrease. Once our small-group conferences are edging closer and closer to ten minutes, we can add another one-to-one conference to our daily plan.

Monday	Tuesday	Wednesday	Thursday	Friday
5-minute 1–1	5-minute 1–1	5-minute 1–1	5-minute 1–1	5-minute 1–1
10-minute small-group work	10-minute small-group work	10-minute small-group work	10-minute small-group work	10-minute small-group work
5-minute 1–1	5-minute 1–1	5-minute 1–1	5-minute 1–1	5-minute 1–1

Courtney Claud and Tracy Smith, fourth-grade teachers at Rawlings Elementary (the writing demonstration school in our district), recently co-facilitated a staff development training session with me. Here's the daily conferring structure they shared with the participants.

Monday	Tuesday	Wednesday	Thursday	Friday
5-minute 1–1	5-minute 1–1	5-minute 1–1	5-minute 1–1	5-minute 1–1
10-minute small-group work	10-minute small-group work	10-minute small-group work	10-minute small-group work	10-minute small-group work
10-minute small-group work	10-minute small-group work	10-minute small-group work	10-minute small-group work	10-minute small-group work

Their daily goal of a one-to-one conference and two small-group conferences allows them to meet with between eight and eleven students on any given day. Does that *always* happen? No. But *most* days it does.

Other teachers prefer to have certain days of the week for certain kinds of conferences.

Monday	Tuesday	Wednesday	Thursday	Friday
1–1 (5 minutes)	Table group 1	Skill group 1	Expectation group 1	Progress Group 1
1–1 (5 minutes)	(10 minutes)	(10 minutes)	(10 minutes)	(10 minutes)
1–1 (5 minutes)	Table group 2	Skill group 2	Expectation group 2	Progress Group 2
1–1 (5 minutes)	(10 minutes)	(10 minutes)	(10 minutes)	(10 minutes)
1–1 (5 minutes)	Table group 3	Skill group 3	Expectation group 3	Progress Group 3
	(10 minutes)	(10 minutes)	(10 minutes)	(10 minutes)

The possibilities are endless, and there's no one best plan. What works best for someone else may not be best for you. What is important is that you have a plan for conferring with individuals and small groups that meets the needs of your students. Many of you will probably try several structures, notice what works and what doesn't, and come up with your own version.

Record Keeping

We also need to know with whom we've conferred, how many times, about what, and with whom we still need to confer. Recently, in a seminar on conferring, I asked the teachers to turn and talk about their record-keeping system. When we regrouped, fourth-grade teacher Suzanne shared her thoughts without apology: "I don't take conference notes anymore. I used to write and write and write after conferences, and I never looked at what I wrote again. It just wasn't useful to me."

I couldn't agree more. Why? is one of the first questions most people want answered when learning something, buying something, or trying something.

How will this benefit me? The answer is of utmost importance, especially to teachers. If we are going to take precious time, of which we have so little, to do something, there must be a purpose.

Forming Accountable Groups

A progress conference I described in Chapter 9 (the one making the teaching point that writers are brave spellers) grew out of my records of strategies and skills I'd taught that class. Notes from prior conferences can also reveal patterns that help us form future skill groups.

Showing That We Care

One year, our district held a celebration for students whose writing had been accepted for publication in the *Cross Creek Chronicle,* a juried yearly anthology of student writing. After I had called all the names and given out the certificates, Mandy raised her hand. "You didn't call my name," she said. I stood there frozen. Mandy sat there all smiles. Her mother sat next to her, proud as she could be. And I had to say four awful words that haunt me to this day: "What is your name?" I had worked in Mandy's class. Several times. And the name of this adorable brown-haired, skinny-legged kid with a smile that lit up a room escaped me. I will never forget Mandy's reply. "You don't remember my name?" I wanted the media center floor to open and swallow me up. I felt horrible. Terrible. Awful. I walked up to her, gave her a huge hug, and apologized. She only wanted me to remember her name.

It matters to kids when we call them by name. It matters even more when we remember the titles of their stories, the details in those stories. We send I care messages when we meet with our students in small groups and are able to remember and say a few words about their stories.

Briefing Parents and School Personnel

When we talk about students with parents, colleagues, and administrators, our anecdotal records help us describe the goals and fruits of our work in specific ways. We can tell parents concrete things they can do to support their child's writing development at home. We can document a child's growth as a writer by showing her parents samples from her writing portfolio.

In our district, students are grouped into three tiers (perhaps the spelling should be *tears*?): the lowest third, the middle third, and the highest third. We have whole departments and teams studying student progress.

Recently, I listened to a district employee explain our tier system in great detail to our group of reading and writing staff developers. She mentioned her disappointment during one intervention meeting after another when she asks the classroom teacher what the child struggles with. The response is usually a single word: *reading*. When she follows up with, "Can you say more about that? What is the child struggling with in reading?" the teacher is rarely able to give specifics.

At meetings with building administrators and other district personnel, we teachers can use our record-keeping notes to communicate children's progress (or lack of progress) in very specific ways: we can call them by name; we can list the skills we've been targeting; and we can specify the frequency of our work in small-group and one-to-one conferences. (The frequency of our conferences with students isn't only helpful information, it's often mandated.)

Making It Right for Us

For me, anecdotal records must be useful, of course. However, that isn't my only criterion. For instance, I think working out in a gym is useful. I have friends who go to the gym all the time, who make good use of their membership. But I'm also a believer in quick and efficient. Going to a gym, for me, is neither quick nor efficient. First it takes me a while to get ready—coordinate my outfit, brush my hair. Then I have to drive to the gym, show my card at the front desk, change into my sweats . . . you get the picture. At home, I throw on my sweats and work out. I can commit to working out every day as long as it helps keep me fit and it's quick and efficient. If I had to go to the gym every day to work out, it wouldn't happen.

Many of you are probably thinking just the opposite. *Is she crazy? I wouldn't work out if I didn't belong to a gym!* And that's the point. You have to decide: What are the things my system of conferring must have and not have for *me* to do it every day? Put a record-keeping system in place that works for you. Only you know your strengths. Only you know your quirks. What is essential with record keeping is that you keep records and use them.

Some Possible Approaches

I suggest beginning each week with a single sheet of empty boxes (the number of boxes matches the number of students in the class), then filling in the boxes as we confer with individuals and small groups. Day after day, we fill more boxes, and the empty boxes help us plan our conferring work, both individual and small group, during the week. In a week's time, we ensure that we have met with each student in our class. Here's an example:

Writing Conference Notes, Week of 1/11–1/15				
Dennandra	**Jozelle**	**Nicholas**	**Victoria**	**Payne**
1/11 TC Add a buddy sentence Black snake		1/12 SG Begin story with a sound word rather than "one day . . ." Trampoline		
Miles	**Jake**	**Amber**	**Max**	**Riley**
1/12 SG Begin story with a sound word rather than "one day . . ." New baseball team		1/11 TC Add a buddy sentence New boat		
Christian	**Kyle**	**Jordan**	**Skye**	**Sierra**
1/12 SG Begin story with a sound word rather than "one day . . ." Bike ride home	1/11 TC Add a buddy sentence Caught a fish		1/12 SG Begin story with a sound word rather than "one day . . ." Nana's beach condo	
Shandon	**Hannah**	**Hank**	**Delaney**	**Ryan**
		1/11 TC Add a buddy sentence Football practice		1/11 OTO Use exclamation point to show excitement Rode rollercoaster

What I like about this record-keeping system is that once we create the table and add the students' names, we can make lots of copies and keep them on a clipboard or in a folder. Then when we want to study one student's progress or history—Hank, let's say—we just flip through a stack of forms, looking at Hank's box—third column, fourth row.

Which leads to what to put in the box. For me it has to be quick: the date and type of conference, the teaching point, and the content of the piece. The notes in the boxes give me a lot of information. On Monday, 1/11, I met with Amber, Hank, Kyle, and Dennandra in a table conference. I taught them that writers often write a sentence and add a buddy sentence telling a little bit more about the sentence before. I also jotted down the topic of each of their stories to help me remember. That same day, I met with Ryan in one-to-one conference (OTO). On Tuesday, 1/12, I met with Nicholas, Miles, Christian, and Skye in a skill group (SG).

If I had a one-to-one conference with Kyle the following day, I might begin like this: "How's it going, Kyle? Are you still working on the story about the moment you caught a fish and ended up being published in the fishing magazine?" And I didn't have to include all that information in Kyle's box. "Caught a fish" is enough to help me remember those other important details about Kyle's story.

The empty boxes also give me information. They're a reminder that I need to fill them up by the end of the week. The empty boxes help me refine my research and study closely the students with whom I've *yet* to meet, noticing patterns and deciding *how* I'll meet with them—skill conferences, table conferences, one-to-one conferences, progress conferences, or expectation conferences.

Many teachers have taken this record-keeping form a step further by placing the names of the three or four neediest students on the back of the sheet two more times. This serves as a visual reminder to meet with those students two to three times as often as the rest of the class. When all of the boxes (front and back) are filled, we've met our goal for the week!

Another way to keep records is to make a table like the one shown in Figure 10.1, with specific skills and expectations listed across the top. Researching the room, we then enter the following codes in the boxes:

+ = strong evidence   √ = some evidence   0 = no evidence

	Build Stamina	Be in the Moment	Build Tension	Show, Not Tell	
Dennandra				0	
Jozelle				+	
Nicholas				√ 1/11 — SG Flag on bike	
Payne				0	
Miles				√ 1/11 — SG Fed key deer	
Jake				+	
Amber				+	
Max				√ 1/11 — SG New electric scooter	
Riley				0	
Christian				0	
Kyle				0	
Jordan				0	
Skye				√ 1/11 — SG Played at Nana's	

Figure 10.1 Record Keeping (*continues*)

Figure 10.1 *(continued)*

	Build Stamina	Be in the Moment	Build Tension	Show, Not Tell	
Sierra				0	
Shandon				+	
Hannah				+	
Hank				+	
Delaney				0	
Ryan				+	

Later, we can form groups according to the patterns we notice, targeting our instruction in these skills and expectations. (Remember, the teaching point is already listed on the box!)

In the example in Figure 10.1, I researched the room, looking at the degree to which students were showing, not telling in their stories. Noticing that Max, Miles, Skye, and Nicholas all exhibited some evidence of the skill, I met with them as a group to help them strengthen their ability to do this.

Also, notice that the fifth column is blank. This lets us notice and record skills and strategies that haven't been predetermined. We're teachers, after all. We expect the unexpected.

Having Learned, Do

Using one of the conferring schedules suggested in this chapter or creating one of your own, plan a week's worth of small-group and one-to-one conferences. Write your plan down and carry it with you as you confer. Then, record these conferences, again using one of the systems here or creating your own. At week's end, reflect on your work. How did it go? Were you able to meet the goals you set?

Based on this week's work, ask yourself the following questions:

- Are the goals I've set attainable for me and for my students at this time? Are they too ambitious? Are they not ambitious enough?
- Did I keep records of my conferences with students?
- What can I do to make sure my conference records help me think about my students and their needs?
- Was I able to meet with all of my students at least once during the week?
- Are there ways I can use the time I have to meet the needs of even more of my students?

Your answers to these questions will lead you to think deeply about and explore ways to plan and record small-group work that meet the diverse needs of the students in your writing workshop.

Troubleshooting

FAQs

How do I find time to fit it all in?

Ah, the elusive quality of time. Any troubleshooting chapter in a book for educators has to deal with the problem of time. There is little more time to be had and certainly no more time to give. In the Introduction to this book I made a promise: This is a book about working smarter, not harder. Use the time you already have allotted each day for the write-and-confer portion of the writing workshop for both small-group and one-to-one conferences.

At first, expect your conferences to run a little long. How well I remember the first time I drove a stick shift: how long it took me to put the car in first gear, then s-l-o-w-l-y push down on the gas pedal and at the same time s-l-o-w-l-y release the clutch pedal, all the while listening to the loud revving of the engine, only having to start all over again when I lifted the clutch pedal too quickly and my car lunged forward and died. But it wasn't too long before I was shifting, downshifting, and speeding off from my spot when the light turned green without even thinking about gears or pedals. I could concentrate on the road! (I think I heard the entire population of Seminole, Florida, sigh in relief.)

So your conferences run a little long. Do fewer of them at first. And once you can fly through them without even thinking of the structure, you'll free your mind to think of more important things—What am I going to teach them? How will I do that? You can then work more conferences into your workshops. The time you take now getting familiar with small-group conferences will be time well spent. You'll be able to meet with more kids more often then you ever imagined possible. Allow yourself time to learn, time to practice, and time to improve. (Revisit Chapter 10 for some recommendations on ways to plan and implement small-group work.)

What are the other students doing?

This is one of the questions I am asked most frequently: "What do I do with the other kids while I am conducting small-group and one-to-one conferences?" The answer is simple: They write!

Your students should be doing the work of writers—independently working on an ongoing project related to the current unit. Teach your students from day one that these are your expectations. Then ask yourself, "Is my whole class having trouble with this?" If so, reteach your expectations in a whole-class minilesson. Show the students what it is you want them to do. Have a group of students demonstrate the way they sit at their seats and write and write and write. As they do, specifically state what it is you want your students to notice. "Notice the way they are all sitting with their feet on the floor? Notice their pencils are moving across the page. Watch Brandon. He finished one story. Now he's getting another story booklet. That's what we do during workshop." If you notice most of your kids know what to do during the write-and-confer portion of the workshop, have an expectation conference (see Chapter 8) with the few who are struggling.

Here are a few additional tips I've picked up across the years.

■   *Be a cheerleader.* At the beginning of the year (or any time) rotate quickly through the room, giving kids quick compliments, pats on the back, thumbs-up signals, and huge smiles. "So smart, Rafeal. You finished one entry and now you are moving to the next." "I'm loving the work this whole table is doing. Everyone is sitting, thinking, and writing." I don't use hushed tones for this—I want the other students to hear. If I notice a child who isn't writing or is struggling with an idea, I'll go up to the student sitting next to that child and give him or her a compliment. Say that Tyler, Devyn, Nikki, and Tyrone sit at a table. Nikki is writing up a storm. Tyrone isn't writing anything. I walk up to Nikki and say, "Nikki, I noticed that you sat down and started writing. Good work. Writers do that. We carve out time every day to write and every day we write. Sometimes we struggle to come up with an idea, but we know we have strategies to help us—like those on that chart right there on the wall. If we don't have an idea, we can [I read the strategies listed on the chart]. I know you'll always remember that as a writer, Nikki. Keep going." Tyrone, overhearing, picks up these tips as well.

■ *Expedite transitions.* The way kids move from their workstations to the gathering area sets the tone for how they will act in the gathering area. And the way they move from the gathering area to their independent work areas sets the tone for their independent work. We want these transitions to be quick (so writers have more time to write), and we want them to be calm. We can do this by dismissing kids in small groups at first, as a whole class later. We can also narrate the transitions, pointing out behavior we want our students to emulate. A teacher is in the gathering area with the whole class in front of her. She has just finished her minilesson. "Group 3, it's time to write." These students get up and head toward their seats. "Writers on the rug, watch the way this group is heading toward their seats quickly, silently. I'm especially noticing how they are sitting down and writing right away! They know just what to do during quiet writing time. Group 2, it's time to write. Let's admire the way group 2 does the same thing we noticed group 3 doing. Writers on the rug, give me a thumbs-up if you are noticing, like I am, the way group 2 is doing the same thing group 3 did."

■ *Have materials at the ready.* At the Poynter Institute writers camp, we always have our "campers" take their yellow legal drafting pad out of their writing portfolio before the minilesson. This cuts down on the sounds of paper being shuffled and binders being snapped open. And you know how irritating it is to listen to the wheezy grinding of the pencil sharpener during writing workshop. You might as well scratch your nails across the chalkboard! So keep two coffee cans/baskets/jars in your classroom, one labeled *sharp*, the other *dull*. As a classroom teacher, I designated a "pencil manager" as one of our classroom jobs. This student came to the classroom a few minutes early (or stayed late, if permitted) to get all of the pencils ready for the day. I also had a supply area and kept it stocked. Having the materials at the ready gives children more time to write.

- *Interject important teaching points.* Once in a while, get everyone's attention and highlight something a student or group of students is doing especially well. "Class, pencils down, eyes and ears on me, please. I want to tell you something amazing. Our class has been writing now for about twelve minutes. I noticed that everyone at the purple table sat down and began writing and hasn't stopped writing for twelve minutes. Purple table, hold your pieces up for the class. [Oohs and aahs from their classmates.] Everyone at the purple table knows exactly what to do during workshop. We write!" In the process of giving students a minibreak, you've reinforced a writing strategy.
- *Create strategy charts.* (See Figure 11.1) The best way to teach kids independence is to teach them strategies. It helps to record those strategies on a chart and post them in the room. That way, when kids are stuck and want to remember a strategy, it's right there. (In kindergarten and first grade, include pictures.)
- *Set limits and stick to them.* Students need to understand that although they have choices during the workshop, those choices are not unlimited. We teach students what they can do. And when needed, what they can't do. Giving students choices requires that they act responsibly. Responsibility can be taught. Many teachers use behavior management systems to encourage responsibility in the classroom. If you have such a system, you'll want to use the system throughout the day, to include writing workshop.

Let me wrap up by also saying what I think ought *not* happen in the name of teaching small groups. Don't invent time-killing centers or pass out prompts or other writing worksheets to keep kids "busy" while you teach in small groups. The whole point of teaching your students writing skills, strategies, and techniques is so that they'll do these things independently. How can we expect our kids to do the work independently if we never give them the chance to try? Our students should be working independently *most* of the time and meeting with us for only *some* of that time.

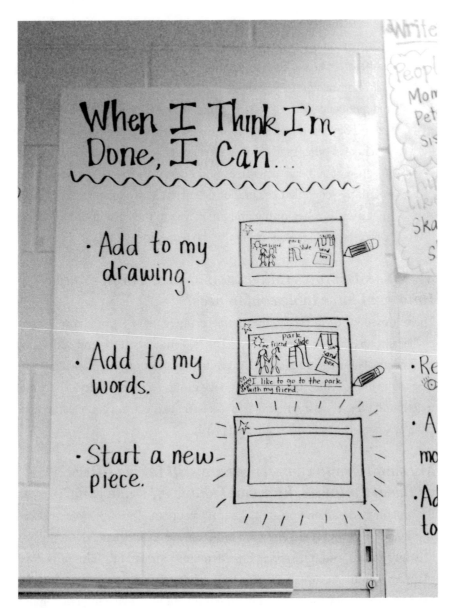

Figure 11.1 Strategy Chart

■ *Make share time bigger.* Because of time constraints, teachers often cut the share time short or pass it up entirely. However, sharing is one of the best methods I know of to promote independence during the workshop. Sometimes, I'll interrupt the class to prepare them for the share. "Writers, in a few moments we'll reconvene back together in the meeting area to share. Will you place a sticky note highlighting a writing strategy or technique you tried today in your writing and be prepared to talk with your group?"

■ *Celebrate regularly.* Regularly scheduled celebrations also promote independence during writing time. Oftentimes, writing celebrations extend beyond the classroom walls. We invite parents, students, and teachers in other grade levels, as well as school community members. A sense of audience energizes our students to write. When we hold regularly scheduled celebrations, our students come to understand that there is a beginning and an ending to the current unit of study. Deadlines bring about energy in the workshop.

My kids sit in rows rather than at tables or in groups. How can I have table conferences?

There are all kinds of classroom seating arrangements—grids, rows, semicircles. Group children by proximity: "The two students at the end of this row and the row behind it are group 1. Anytime I say group 1, you know I'm referring to the four of you." Then you can have group 1 slide their desks or chairs together (if that seems appropriate) or ask them to meet you at the conference table or some other suitable gathering place.

My small-group conferences are still taking fifteen or twenty minutes, how can I shave off some time?

As I mentioned earlier, you should expect your small-group conferences to run long at first. But there are ways to become more efficient. Get a timer—it is invaluable. And remember: Less is more. I know I'm guilty of overexplaining. I think to myself, *In case they didn't get that, let me explain it this way, too.* Then I say the same thing in a different way, believing I'm helping. But it often has the opposite effect. When we overexplain a skill, technique, or strategy, we usually aren't making ourselves more clear but rather confusing children. Think about the teaching part of the conference as three steps: Tell the students what you are going to teach them, show them how you or another writer does it, tell them what you just taught. It's a quick demonstration. It's a *mini*minilesson.

One-to-one coaching around the table often makes a conference run long. Think about the kinds of questions and the level of talk you are having with your students. "Tell me about your piece, Sahara" will prompt a much different response than, "Can you show me where you are trying this work, Sahara?" Because you've most likely already researched the class and studied the work, your questions in a small group can be a little more direct and guided.

How many students should be in a group?
Between three and five students are ideal—more than five and things get helter-skelter. Primary teachers should lean toward the bottom of the range. Upper-grade teachers can move toward the top of the range.

What do I do when one of the children in the group has already done the work I'm teaching?
Sometimes we discover that a child in a group is already proficient in the skill we're teaching. This happens most often with table conferences, when we haven't done any research but are reminding students about something or reteaching a skill. But it can happen in a skill conference as well, either because we were less thorough in our research than we should have been or because the child caught on to something in the meantime. First of all, we should compliment the child! Then we can encourage the student to try the same skill or strategy in other parts of his piece or even in other pieces. "Reece, I'm noticing you did add setting details to your story. Right here you wrote, 'The shopping carts were tucked into one after another after another.' I'm wondering if you can try this strategy in other parts of your story. In fact, you could try adding setting details to every page in your story."

Which kind of teaching is most effective—one on one, small group, or whole class?
Recently, a colleague of mine heard Richard Allington speak about the teaching of reading. He told the group that it is a known fact that one-to-one instruction is better than small group and that small-group instruction is better than whole group. I have also read research that says in some cases small-group instruction may be more effective than individual or whole-group instruction,

because children benefit from listening to their classmates respond and receive feedback from the teacher. I think the question to be asked is not "Which approach is better than the rest?" but rather "How can we organize our time so that we can use them all to our best advantage?"

Tips for Conferring Effectively

Don't Overconfer

At the Poynter Institute writers camps, there is one teacher for every four or five students, and conferring can get out of hand. Because of the favorable teacher–student ratio, it's easy for a child to have more than one conference during a workshop. But as much as we want to meet with our students frequently, it's possible to overdo it. We want to leave students with something to ponder and try on their own and *give them the time to do so*. For our camps, we devised a system based on sticky notes. When a teacher has a conference with a child, she leaves a sticky note at the child's workspace, so the rest of us know not to have another conference with that child. In the same way, teachers in the classroom can leave this kind of visual reminder after they've met with children. You can also try a physical reminder. If you meet with a skill group in the gathering area, leave the group there. Say, "Continue writing right here. I'll come back in a few minutes to marvel at your progress."

Allow for Choice

We teach our kids to be independent—that during writing workshop, everyone writes. We teach our students strategies to use when they are stuck. We teach them that, mostly, we determine when and with whom we confer. That being said, it's not the best idea to be hard-nosed about it. There have been plenty of times in my writing life when I've felt that I cannot write another word until I talk to someone. (It happened as I was writing this book.) Our kids get that way, too. Here are a few ideas to build in some flexibility.

- *Buddy conferences/partnership conferences.* Recently, in a fourth-grade classroom, I saw a wall chart that proclaimed, "Ask three, then me." Rather than immediately ask the teacher, these children knew to ask three peers first. If they didn't get the help they needed that way, they could then go to the teacher. I don't know if I would want children disturbing three kids during a writing workshop, but asking one other student first is an excellent suggestion.

■ In Chapter 8, I describe an expectation conference in which partners who were working particularly well together were given permission to meet at their own discretion and taught procedures for doing so (see page 72). This is another way to help students sustain their writing without relying on us. However, we should set clear expectations and limits. One expectation might be that a student first has to try to solve the problem on her or his own. Limits might include the length of the discretionary conference and the number held per week.

Figure 11.2 Writing Center

■ *The writing center.* (See Figure 11.2) Many teachers have a writing center in their room stocked with paper, scissors, pens, pencils, dictionaries, mentor texts, and any other supplies kids need at the ready when they are writing. Students know they can quietly get the supplies they need when they need them.

Work with Colleagues

Learning is social. Recruit a colleague (or a grade-level team) to try this work alongside you. Our conversations are richer when we have someone besides the voices in our own head with whom to trade ideas and feedback. I have taught in situations where I felt totally alone. Other times I've had the support of a whole team of thinkers, creators, and instigators, who also turned out to be the best of friends. The times when I am surrounded by wonderful colleagues are my times of greatest professional growth. Lean on someone. We are one another's greatest resources. Form a book group at your school or in your district. Ask your principal, learning specialist, or curriculum support person to supply copies of the books the group studies. Most principals will scrape up a few extra dollars to support professional growth for the willing and eager.

Build and Nurture Relationships

Not long ago, I took a handful of colleagues to a school in my district. We visited three classrooms, and I demonstrated different types of small-group instruction as my colleagues watched and took notes. In the last classroom, I joined a table of five third-grade writers. I began the conversation with the children just as I had in the first two classrooms, getting the attention of the group and paying a compliment. Then I taught them a variation of the day's minilesson on writing a "background lead." The conference was a disaster. As I coached each writer at the table individually, I could tell he or she couldn't wait for me to move on. No matter how hard I tried, the children weren't responding to my instruction. One child stared at his notebook. Another child covered her face and mouth with her hands when I approached her to talk. Only one child in the group of five, Manuel, was open, eager, and responsive. My colleagues observed the group interaction (or lack thereof) with pity.

Later, we discussed the day. The first two demonstrations had gone smoothly: the children responded, tried out the work, produced a ton of writing, and proudly shared their work. What had gone wrong in the third classroom? What had been different? Through a process of elimination, we determined that I did not have a relationship with the children in the third classroom. I didn't know their names and they didn't know mine. They didn't trust me. How could they know they were free to take risks and try new things? That I was there to support and encourage them, not ridicule or shame them? They didn't.

Except Manuel. Why had Manuel responded to my instruction the way he did? When I approached Manuel, I asked him how it was going. He responded by reading part of his background lead to a gripping story about his first day in third grade. In the lead, he remembered some important background information leading up to his first day: "Last year Jose, my cousin, told me about the third grade FCAT." After he read that line, I asked, "Is Jose Gonzales your cousin?" Manuel nodded proudly. "Jose was my student in third grade," I said, smiling as I remembered Jose and his little sister Natalia and the day his mother and grandmother came in to celebrate his birthday with balloons and cake only to have to wait out in the hallway until we finished the dreaded FCAT testing.

Manuel responded to my teaching that day because, by coincidence, we connected and began to form a relationship. Manuel opened the door and invited me in. Manuel and the other children in his class are a constant reminder to me of how critical it is for teachers to form and nurture relationships with students, especially during small-group instruction. Students need to learn to trust us and one another.

Final Thoughts

Our state requires each district to adopt a new reading program every five years. Recently, I attended back-to-back presentations made by representatives of two large publishing companies. The presentations were top-notch and included all the bells and whistles—PowerPoint presentations, three-ring binders, tabs telling us exactly where to turn when. We were even given gift bags with pens, notebooks, and similar "swag." The presenters were extremely proud of their products. They spent a lot of time highlighting the step-by-step "foolproof" lesson plans:

- You teach skill X on this day.
- If you have kids in the blah-blah-blah range, you follow up by using the blue-coded books. The green-coded books are for students who fall into the blah-blah-blah range.
- On Tuesday, you'll introduce this concept by saying. . . .
- Notice the two columns? The first column is for teachers with experience. The second column is for new teachers.
- Behind the red tab are lessons for kids needing extra support.
- The workbook is for. . . .

Both programs even had built-in writing programs! (Don't get me started on that.)

I was a little disturbed by all of it. This is what it has come to? This is what is being marketed to teachers? Neither presentation mentioned the word *think*. Thinking didn't seem to be required of the teacher at all. There were no decisions to be made. The publishing companies had thought of everything.

This is scary. I worry about what it says about our profession. We are teachers. It is our job to teach others to think. But the message is clear. *We are not required to think.* Because we don't have time. Beware the curriculum designed so that we don't have to think, if for no reason other than this: Your mail carrier, the teenaged kid who bags your groceries, or the person behind the counter at any convenience store could get up in front of kids and teach it. *Anyone* could.

My hope is that the information and ideas presented in this book have generated lots of *thinking* on your part. Sometimes you were thinking, *Yes. That makes sense.* Other times it was, *Hmm, I don't know if I agree with that.* If you have put these ideas into practice, you've no doubt met with some frustration (although I hope with success as well). But that is what teaching is all about: growing professionally by trying new methods, ideas, and suggestions and finding what works for you and your students. My greatest hope is that the information in this book has caused lots of collegial conversation in book groups, in the teachers' lounge, at after-school get-togethers.

Good teaching takes time and energy. It takes the willingness to try and the passion to keep at it. It takes thoughtfulness and robust, searching conversations. And a good sense of humor always helps. I wish you all of those things.

References

Anderson, Carl. 2000. *How's It Going? A Practical Guide to Conferring with Student Writers.* Portsmouth, NH: Heinemann.

———. 2005. *Assessing Writers.* Portsmouth, NH: Heinemann.

Calkins, Lucy. 1994. *The Art of Teaching Writing.* 2nd ed. Portsmouth, NH: Heinemann.

———. 2006. *A Guide to the Writing Workshop,* Units of Study for Teaching Writing, Grades 3–5. Portsmouth, NH: *first*hand, Heinemann.

Calkins, Lucy, Amanda Hartman, and Zoe White. 2005. *One to One: The Art of Conferring with Young Writers.* Portsmouth, NH: Heinemann.

Calkins, Lucy, et al. 2006. *Units of Study for Teaching Writing, Grades 3–5.* 7 vols. Portsmouth, NH: *first*hand, Heinemann.

———. 2007. *Units of Study for Primary Writing: A Yearlong Curriculum (Grades K–2).* 7 vols. Portsmouth, NH: *first*hand, Heinemann.

Clark, Roy P. 2006. *Writing Tools: 50 Essential Strategies for Every Writer.* New York: Little Brown.

DuFour, Richard, Robert Eaker, and Rebecca DuFour. 2005. *On Common Ground: The Power of Professional Learning Communities.* Bloomington, IN: National Education Service.

Fletcher, Ralph. 1993. *What a Writer Needs.* Portsmouth, NH: Heinemann.

Fletcher, Ralph, and Joann Portalupi. 1998. *Craft Lessons.* York, ME: Stenhouse.

Gliori, Debi. 1999. *No Matter What.* Great Britain: Bloomsbury Publishing Plc.

Graves, Donald. 1994. *A Fresh Look at Writing.* Portsmouth, NH: Heinemann.

———. 1983, 2003. *Writing: Teachers and Children at Work.* Portsmouth, NH: Heinemann.

———. 2006. *A Sea of Faces: The Importance of Knowing Your Students.* Portsmouth, NH: Heinemann.

Graves, Donald H., and Penny Kittle. 2005. *Inside Writing: How to Teach the Details of Craft.* Portsmouth, NH: Heinemann.

Greenfield, Eloise. 1974. *She Come Bringing Me That Little Baby Girl.* Illustrated by John Steptoe. New York: Harper Trophy.

———. 1978. *Honey, I Love and Other Love Poems.* New York. Harper Collins.

Heard, Georgia. 1998. *Awakening the Heart: Exploring Poetry in Elementary and Middle School.* Portsmouth, NH: Heinemann.

Keats, Ezra J. 1967. *Peter's Chair.* New York: Harper and Row.

———. 1968. *A Letter to Amy.* New York: Harper and Row.

Laminack, Lester, and Reba Wadsworth. 2006. *Learning Under the Influence of Language and Literature: Making the Most of Read-Alouds Across the Day.* Portsmouth, NH: Heinemann.

Mermelstein, Leah. 2005. *Reading/Writing Connections in the K–2 Classroom: Find the Clarity and Then Blur the Lines.* Boston: Allyn & Bacon.

Murray, Donald M. 1985. *A Writer Teaches Writing.* Boston: Houghton Mifflin.

Ray, Katie Wood. 1999. *Wondrous Words.* Urbana, IL: NCTE.

———. 2002. *What You Know by Heart.* Portsmouth, NH: Heinemann.

———. 2006. *Study Driven: A Framework for Planning Units of Study in the Writing Workshop.* Portsmouth, NH: Heinemann.

Ray, Katie Wood, and Lester Laminack. 2001. *The Writing Workshop: Working Through the Hard Parts (And They're All Hard Parts).* Urbana, IL: NCTE.

Williams, Vera. 1982. *A Chair for My Mother.* New York: Greenwillow.

Yolen, Jane. 1987. *Owl Moon.* Illustrated by John Schoenherr. New York: Philomel.